## ULI Project Staff

**Rachelle L. Levitt**
*Executive Vice President, Policy and Practice*
*Publisher*

**Ann Oliveri**
*Senior Vice President for Strategic Development*

**Janine Pesci**
*Managing Director, Programs and Customized Education*

**Trisha Riggs**
*Managing Director, Communications*
*Project Director*

**Hugh Broadus**
*Senior Associate, Communications*

**Nancy Stewart**
*Director, Book Program*

**Carol A. Bell**
*Copy Editor*

**Betsy Van Buskirk**
*Art Director*

**Susan S. Teachey/ON-Q Design, Inc.**
*Layout/Design*

**Craig Chapman**
*Director, Publishing Operations*

## About the ULI Leadership Development Initiative

Identifying best practices and sharing experience

The Leadership Development Initiative identifies, challenges, and develops members as leaders of their professions, industries, communities, and the Institute.

# LEADERSHIP LEGACIES

## LESSONS LEARNED FROM TEN REAL ESTATE LEGENDS

EDITOR
Trisha Riggs

AUTHORS
Desiree French
Mike Sheridan

Urban Land Institute

## About ULI—the Urban Land Institute

ULI–the Urban Land Institute is a nonprofit education and research institute that is supported by its members. Its mission is to provide responsible leadership in the use of land in order to enhance the total environment.

ULI sponsors educational programs and forums to encourage an open international exchange of ideas and sharing of experiences; initiates research that anticipates emerging land use trends and issues and proposes creative solutions based on that research; provides advisory services; and publishes a wide variety of materials to disseminate information on land use and real estate development. Each year, the Institute honors an extraordinary community builder through the Urban Land Institute J.C. Nichols Prize for Visionaries in Urban Development.

Established in 1936, the Institute today has more than 24,000 members from 80 countries representing the entire spectrum of land use and development disciplines.

**Richard M. Rosan**
*President*

Recommended bibliographic listing

Riggs, Trisha, Desiree French, and Mike Sheridan. *Leadership Legacies: Lessons Learned from Ten Real Estate Legends.* Washington, D.C.: ULI–the Urban Land Institute, 2004.

ULI Catalog Number: L12
International Standard Book Number: 0-87420-932-3
Library of Congress Control Number: 2004099416

# Contents

**Foreword** . . . . . . . . . . . . . . . . . . . . . . . . . . . . . . . . . . . . . . . . . . . . .vi
Harry H. Frampton III

**Acknowledgments** . . . . . . . . . . . . . . . . . . . . . . . . . . . . . . . . . . . . .ix

**Chapter One** . . . . . . . . . . . . . . . . . . . . . . . . . . . . . . . . . . . . . . . . .2
Trammell Crow:
   Transforming the Business Model

**Chapter Two** . . . . . . . . . . . . . . . . . . . . . . . . . . . . . . . . . . . . . . . . .10
Charles E. Fraser:
   Living the Vision

**Chapter Three** . . . . . . . . . . . . . . . . . . . . . . . . . . . . . . . . . . . . . . .18
James Graaskamp:
   Reinventing Real Estate Education

**Chapter Four** . . . . . . . . . . . . . . . . . . . . . . . . . . . . . . . . . . . . . . . .26
Gerald D. Hines:
   Creating the Culture

**Chapter Five** . . . . . . . . . . . . . . . . . . . . . . . . . . . . . . . . . . . . . . . .36
James Rouse:
   Leading from the Heart

**Chapter Six** . . . . . . . . . . . . . . . . . . . . . . . . . . . . . . . . . . . . . . . . .44
Stephen B. Siegel:
   Listening and Learning

**Chapter Seven** . . . . . . . . . . . . . . . . . . . . . . . . . . . . . . . . . . . . . .52
Donald Terner:
   Bridging the Gap in Low-Income Housing

**Chapter Eight** . . . . . . . . . . . . . . . . . . . . . . . . . . . . . . . . . . . . . . .60
Robert Venturi and Denise Scott Brown:
   Collaborating for Success

**Chapter Nine** . . . . . . . . . . . . . . . . . . . . . . . . . . . . . . . . . . . . . . . .72
Sam Zell:
   Investing in People

**Appendix 1**      Bibliography . . . . . . . . . . . . . . . . . . . . . . . . . . . . .81

**Appendix 2**      ULI Leadership Development Initiative . . . . . . . . . . . . . . .82

# Foreword

Straightforward. Ethical. Trustworthy. Excellent listener. Humble. Passionate. Committed. Decisive. Courageous. Gutsy. Open-minded. Self-aware. Interested. Inclusive. Supportive.

Are these qualities characteristic of current leadership in the land use industry? How can these traits be passed on to the next generation of land use leaders and community builders? What can today's leaders teach those who will be leading the industry in the years ahead?

As chairman of the Urban Land Institute, one of my priorities has been for the Institute to offer tools that foster the development of leadership skills. In December 2003, ULI convened a Leadership Roundtable of 30 real estate executives to discuss the characteristics of effective leaders and explore what the Institute could best do to foster leadership skills.

While the roundtable covered a wide range of leadership development topics, participants concurred that the basis for any corporate leadership track is creating a culture of openness and trust—characteristics that often are overshadowed by drive and assertiveness in the highly competitive land use and development industry. However, taking the time to create such a culture and provide leadership opportunities to those moving up makes the difference between short-term and long-term success, they noted.

In *Leadership Legacies: Lessons Learned from Ten Real Estate Legends*, ULI matches the attributes that members believe define a good leader with some of the most inspiring professionals in the land use industry: Trammell Crow, who changed the development business model; Charles Fraser, who lived his vision; James Graaskamp, who challenged the conventions of real estate education; Gerald D. Hines, who created a culture of excellence; James Rouse, who led from the heart; Steve Siegel, who listens and learns; Don Terner, who did whatever it took; Robert Venturi and Denise Scott-Brown, who collaborate for success; and Sam Zell, who invests in people.

Although their careers are widely varied, these individuals share some common traits of exceptional leaders—an ability to think creatively and think long term; to recognize potential unseen by others; to listen; and, perhaps most important, to learn from others and to share their own knowledge. They have raised the bar for the rest of us.

Each profile in Leadership Legacies is centered around a lesson that all of us can use to improve the environment in which people live, work and play. The story of my mentor, Charles Fraser, focuses on his development philosophy, which was to "create a way of life, not just build a subdivision." Forty years ago, Charles instilled in me, and many others, a lasting commitment to strive for the best and never to settle for "just good enough." I'm sure many of you can also name at least one individual who has made a lasting, profound difference in the path you have chosen: someone who was inspirational, who was willing to take risks in pursuit of excellence; and whose perseverance ultimately resulted in better buildings, better neighborhoods and better communities. This level of  influence and impact can be found in each Leadership Legacies profile. These are stories that illustrate what it takes to create positive change.

To build the best communities, we must be effective, persuasive community leaders with fresh ideas. Being equipped with the best market information and the best business strategy is not enough to make better communities a reality. The most critical component is leadership.

As ULI members and land use professionals, we need to demonstrate the leadership skills necessary to attract, motivate, and retain the best and brightest minds—the land use leaders of the future. Indeed, if we are to appeal to those who are straightforward, ethical, trustworthy, humble, passionate, committed, gutsy, open-minded, curious, inclusive, courageous, and supportive, we have to lead by example. And for inspiration, we need to look no further than the ten real estate legends featured in the pages ahead.

**Harry H. Frampton III**
*Chairman, Urban Land Institute*

# Acknowledgments

## Advisory Group Reviewers

Anthony LoPinto, Chairman
Managing Director and CEO
Equinox Partners
New York, New York

Dorothy Alpert
National Managing Director for Real Estate, Hospitality, and
Construction Service
Deloitte
New York, New York

Michael J. Bush, Esq.
Executive Director
REAP–The Real Estate Associate Program
Washington, D.C.

Phil Harkins
CEO
Linkage, Inc.
Burlington, Massachusetts

Peter McMahon
President
Kennecott Land Company
Salt Lake City, Utah

Michael  Rodis
Senior Vice President, Human Resources
The Mills Corporation
Arlington, Virginia

Charlene Rothkopf
Executive Vice President, Human Resources
AvalonBay Communities
Alexandria, Virginia

## Dedication

*To the thousands of people whose careers and lives were forever changed by these extraordinary leaders—and who today are carrying on their legacies. The built environment is all the better for it.*

# LEADERSHIP LEGACIES

## LESSONS LEARNED FROM TEN REAL ESTATE LEGENDS

# CHAPTER ONE

# TRAMMELL CROW:
## Transforming the Business Model

Desiree French

### LEADERSHIP LESSON
### Leaders create more leaders.

"A group of people, working closely together, can provide the deliverables of direction, ensuring competence and ensuring that change is implemented. To do so requires participants to share similar values, to develop a commitment to each other and the organization, and to allow those who possess complementary skills to lead when appropriate."

*Leading for a Change: How to Master the 5 Challenges Faced by Every Leader*—Ralph D. Jacobson, Keith Setterholm, and John Vollum

In national and international real estate circles, the Trammell Crow Company stands out as one of the top commercial real estate services companies in the United States.

The man who made it all possible is Trammell Crow, the company's legendary founder who started out more than 55 years ago building industrial warehouses in Dallas. He went on to grace the landscape with the likes of the deluxe Anatole Hotel in Dallas, Peachtree Center in Atlanta, Embarcadero Center in San Francisco, and Dallas Market Center, the largest wholesale trade and merchandise mart in the world.

In the 1970s and 1980s, the Trammell Crow Company was the largest commercial developer in the country. It attained that distinction based on a unique and powerful corporate culture that embraced a spirit of entrepreneurialism and trust.

> **"I believe [he] is the father of the partnership structure in real estate. He probably has created more partners, who have created more wealth in real estate, than anyone else."**

Crow, a visionary and risk taker who surrounded himself with very capable people—specifically, young people with fire in their bellies—pioneered the concept of speculative real estate development. But he is, perhaps, noted most for creating partnerships to build projects rather than adhering to a traditional corporate organizational structure.

"I believe [he] is the father of the partnership structure in real estate," says Ron Terwilliger, national managing partner of Trammell Crow Residential and a former ULI chairman. "He probably has created more partners, who have created more wealth in real estate, than anyone else."

And for that, his former partners are eternally grateful. Hundreds have achieved huge financial success and security. But, more important, they were given the opportunity of a lifetime, while in their 20s and 30s, to become partners in the fastest growing show in town. In exchange for extremely low salaries at the outset, many were able to reap hefty future

**Crow (standing, middle) at Mercantile Bank "praying for a loan" for Trade Mart in 1957, with colleagues Storey Stemmons (left) and John Stemmons (right).**

*Courtesy of the Crow family*

rewards and eventually move on to create their own companies and organizations.

"He spawned a whole generation or two of very successful real estate people. Many of them today are great leaders all over the country," says Ned Spieker, one of those former partners who, today, is managing partner of Spieker Partners, Inc., in Menlo Park, California. He is also the former chairman of Spieker Properties, Inc., an office-industrial real estate investment trust purchased by Equity Office Properties for $7.3 billion in 2001.

Spieker was 25 when Crow made him a general partner more than two decades ago. He remained with the company for 17 years. "The lesson I learned from Trammell," says Spieker, "was to share. The only way you can build a large business is to share the profits and the glory. You have to create trusted leaders that you treat on an equal plane. I took that principle from Trammell and applied it in my own companies."

Crow's strategy was simple but innovative. After developing industrial projects in Dallas, he ventured into other parts of the country in the mid-1960s and began to diversify his portfolio. To expand his reach, he built the business using capital and operational partners.

Crow gave his partners, who opened offices for him around the country, meaningful ownership shares in the projects, not just lip service. They shared in the equity of a building and the decentralization of the organization, allowing them to have tremendous control.

He recognized that ownership was a very powerful incentive to monitor expenses and maximize profits.

The partnerships, as one former partner put it, were a "rising tide business." If one of his partnerships did well, then Crow also did well. If one did not, he had to ride along with the tide.

**"The only way you can build a large business is to share the profits and the glory. You have to create trusted leaders that you treat on an equal plane. I took that principle from Trammell and applied it in my own companies."**

Crow was different from other executives in that he met with his young recruits, many of whom were leasing agents—on the first rung on the partnership ladder—during their first interviews at his company. But he did not ask the typical interview questions. He would ask someone about his relationship with his father and whether the recruit was a churchgoer—questions generally considered taboo today.

"He was more interested in the composition of the individual. Trammell looked for someone with brains who was a good guy," says Jon Hammes, a former partner and now managing partner with Hammes Company, a development firm in Milwaukee. "He wanted to be associated with people who would succeed."

Eventually, some in the real estate industry began to refer to Crow's partners as "clones" because they all had something in common with Crow and with each other. They shared the fundamental and very intangible attributes that Trammell sought—high personal standards and sound character, a strong work ethic, enormous energy, and an entrepreneurial spirit.

"The principles and entrepreneurial spirit that Trammell fathered have molded many of us as we have gone on to establish our own companies and organizations," continues Hammes. "Those principles include employing the type of people you build a company around, using the concept of meritocracy, making ownership possible, having ethical standards, and building an organization where people are more

**Crow (middle) watches as stock in the Trammell Crow Company is opened to the public on the New York Stock Exchange in November 1997.**

*Courtesy of the Crow family*

than just employees. The model he mentored me on is a sound model. It has worked for me in my own business."

During its heyday in the mid-1980s, the Trammell Crow Company was hiring 125 master of business administration graduates per year, up from a mere one or two in the early 1970s. At one point, Crow had more than 600 partnerships.

His partners were a loyal bunch. When Crow ran out of money and was hit hard by rising interest rates, mounting debt, and a glut of office buildings and other real estate in the mid-1970s, his partners rallied to the rescue and anted up $100 million.

"We just sat around in a circle and said we would raise the money and loan it back to him," says Spieker. "That doesn't happen often, but because he created such trust among the partners, he just called on us and we came to his aid. There was a great deal of love there."

It was an example of the very powerful bond that Crow had forged, one that was truly unique in comparison to other organizations. The partners shared a strong sense of brotherhood. It was something that Crow had personally cultivated within the organization. The partners were partners in the truest sense of the word.

In fact, when Crow once spoke at the Harvard Business School, he was asked to identify the most important element in creating a successful organization. He replied that it was "love."

"Trammell believed in that, and he felt that if you had a general sense of love for people you would be more successful than not. And if you believed in what you were doing, you would be more successful," says Hammes. "He created a culture that I don't know has ever been replicated."

Crow is said to have put forth to all his employees a fatherly or grandfatherly disposition, whether they were secretaries or accountants. "He was not the aggressive, pin-you-to-a-corner type. On the other hand, he was not a fool either. If you got on the wrong side of him, it could be taxing," says Bob Kresko, a former Crow partner who has a part ownership in Krombach Partners, an affiliate of a real estate brokerage business in St. Louis. "The great thing about Trammell is that you didn't have to agree with him 100 percent in order to work with him."

> **"Trammell . . . felt that if you had a general sense of love for people you would be more successful than not. And if you believed in what you were doing, you would be more successful."**

# Trammell Crow

## BIOGRAPHY

At 89, Trammell Crow has, by all accounts, lived a full life as a humble yet extraordinary entrepreneur. But besides developing properties and establishing himself as an icon in real estate, the former Navy commander has been equally fond of collecting Asian art, particularly jade, of which he has accumulated more than 1,200 artifacts.

Some even quip that Crow went into the hotel business—he built the upscale Anatole Hotel in Dallas and founded the Wyndham Hotel chain—simply to have a place to store his voluminous works of art from Japan, China, and India.

Crow seemed to make purchases of all kinds—a ranch, land, paintings, or sculptures— wherever he traveled. "Trammell never saw a deal he didn't like. He didn't like to say 'No,'" chuckles Ned Spieker.

**In recruiting an employee, Crow sought "someone with brains who was a good guy."**

*Courtesy of the Crow family*

"Trammell knew where the accelerator was, but he never knew where the brakes were."

When Spieker worked in San Francisco, Crow would visit about once every six months, presumably to talk shop. Instead, they would end up in Gump's—a famous retail store that sells exclusive and high-quality merchandise mostly from the Pacific rim—for a behind-closed-doors art sale. Afterwards, Crow would hop into the car and head back to the airport.

A graduate of Dallas public schools and Southern Methodist University, Crow was the fifth of eight children from a lower-middle-income family. Formally trained as an accountant, he had no previous experience in real estate or architecture before setting foot in the real estate arena to help his wife manage a warehouse she had inherited.

Throughout his career, Crow had an exceptional ability to cultivate relationships in the political as well as business and financial arena. He was actively involved in the Republican Party. He supported, and was very close to, George W. Bush and Gerald Ford.

Bob Kresko, a former Crow partner and current part owner of Kromback Partners in St. Louis, was amazed by Crow's intellect, which he says was extensive. He says Crow could be around the likes of Henry Kissinger, Herman Kahn, and Elliott Richardson and still hold his own.

"Other people in the circle would kind of become numb and listen to what Henry Kissinger, for example, had to say. Not Trammell. He engaged them all one on one. They listened to what he had to say," says Kresko.

And his perseverance, particularly in business, was virtually unmatched. "He did everything," says Kresko. "He would go into a building and solicit clients and the building manager would kick him out. He wouldn't go back the next day. He would go back within five minutes."

Crow sought in others what he possessed himself—drive, a will to succeed, and moral standards.

Highly religious, Crow's business philosophy was to do business with someone he could trust, as if on a handshake basis. He often delivered great messages to employees not only about the future of real estate, but also about his ethics. He would tell them they did not have to negotiate a deal to death. It was okay, he said, to leave a few nickels on the table and let the other guy walk away with pride.

Crow, who today is afflicted with Alzheimer's disease, was also more concerned about walking away with what he wanted than acquiring something at the cheapest price. The desire to succeed is what really drove him. Money was just a way he kept score.

CHAPTER TWO

# CHARLES FRASER:
## Living the Vision

Desiree French

## LEADERSHIP LESSON
### See connections.

"The people who can achieve something truly unprecedented
have more than enormous talent and intelligence. They have
original minds. They see things differently. They can spot the
gaps in what we think we know. They have a knack for discov-
ering interesting, important problems, as well as the skills for
solving them. They want to do the next thing, not the last one.
They see connections. Often they have broad interests and
multiple frames of reference. They tend to be deep general-
ists, not narrow specialists. They are not so immersed in one
discipline that they can't find solutions in others. They are
visionaries and problem-solvers. . .(and) they have the tenacity that is so necessary to accomplish anything of value."

*Learning to Lead*—Warren Bennis and Joan Goldsmith

In the late 1950s, word began to circulate about an ebullient and brilliant young man who envisioned turning the barrier island of Hilton Head into a unique resort community for well-heeled vacationers and retirees.

Many thought he was crazy. At the time, neither Hilton Head nor South Carolina were popular vacation destinations. But Charles E. Fraser—daring, confident, and driven by incredibly lofty vision—saw the opportunity of a lifetime: to develop 5,000 acres of land that he named Sea Pines Plantation. The sheer ambition and scale of the development set it apart. But it would also become one of the first developments to incorporate master planning, retention of open space, mixed-use facilities, and the use of creative deed restrictions and covenants to ensure high-quality design—all extremely revolutionary measures back then.

**"There was a great sense of pioneering. It all had a sort of evangelical feel. There was quality and innovation in the [Hilton Head] project with land planning and everything else that we did."**

"He had a belief in what could be done," says Michael Ainslie, former president of the National Trust for Historic Preservation, who once worked for Fraser. "He said, 'We're not just peddling dirt, but creating a community.'"

Fraser's brand of conservation-minded planning, which set aside a tremendous amount of green space, was both legendary and unprecedented. He embraced large-scale community planning with a total commitment to the environment, ever mindful of striking a delicate, harmonious balance between natural settings and manmade ones.

"Environmentalism and the kind of care and protection he championed is so commonplace and overused today that you just couldn't imagine that he started this nearly 50 years ago. It seems so mundane and obvious now," says Peter S. Rummell, a Sea Pines alumnus and chairman and chief executive officer of The St. Joe Company, a real estate development company in Florida.

**A young Charles Fraser keeps step with a Hilton Head alligator.**

*Courtesy of the Fraser family*

Fraser understood the importance of planning, design, and architecture. Indeed, he influenced an entire industry of architects and designers with his use of natural colors and building into wooded areas. Perhaps more than anyone at the time, he successfully brought value to the interior land away from the ocean. The houses at Sea Pines blended elegantly into the natural beauty of the landscape. Golf courses were built near new homes inland. Recreational facilities abound. There were bike trails, tennis courts, swimming, boating, and a high-end playground for children. Residents had vegetable gardens. And Fraser, always in step with, or ahead of, the latest trend, was one of the first developers to hire professional athletes to run sports facilities and design first-rate golf courses.

"He had a history of doing these things, which was linked to him being a prolific reader and being determined to understand his customer," contends ULI chairman Harry H. Frampton III, another Fraser protégé whose real estate development company, East West Partners, is headquartered in Beaver Creek, Colorado. "Many of the things Charles pioneered at Sea Pines became commonplace up and down the seacoast. Everybody seemed to copy it."

Fraser was passionate about quality. He relentlessly pursued it, and in the end, people got what they paid for. This was evident time and again in several projects that his company, Sea Pines, later developed, including Amelia Island Plantation in Florida, Kiawah Island Resort in South Carolina, and the Palmas del Mar resort in Puerto Rico. The same fundamental design and strategies used at Hilton Head were applied to these properties.

At Sea Pines, Fraser consistently emphasized to his young protégés the importance of having high-quality design, great market research, and tremendous value behind everything they did.

As someone who treasured creativity, he recruited a very capable group of young people who have stayed in the real estate industry and become leaders. They were attracted to Sea Pines by Fraser's vision, the quality of his aspirations, and his willingness to accept unconventional ideas. Many arrived touting master of business administration and law degrees from Ivy League schools. Most had no practical real estate experience.

A deep, inquisitive thinker himself, Fraser—who had a unique and uncanny way of looking at things—often picked his young protégés brains for ideas and challenged them to think outside the box. Through the years, he encouraged his young charges to share knowledge and information freely.

"There was a great sense of pioneering. It all had a sort of evangelical feel. There was quality and innovation in the [Hilton Head] project with land planning and everything else that we did," recalls Rummell.

Today, hundreds of Fraser protégés are scattered across the country. Many have seeded their own real estate companies over the past 25 to 40 years, incorporating the principles Fraser taught, and building on the concepts he espoused. "He would be very disappointed if we didn't innovate. He wouldn't have wanted

**"Brilliant, yes. Visionary, yes. Impatient, yes. But, what I remember most was his courage, persistence, and tenacity during the most difficult of times."**

us to play the same old records, to do the same old things," says Jim Mozley, senior vice president of Crescent Resources, LLC, in Bluffton, South Carolina.

**Charles and Mary Fraser at the Charles E. Fraser Bridge dedication in 1999.**

*Courtesy of the Fraser family*

Not surprisingly, Fraser was an information hound and put a high premium on research, one of his passions. An avid reader, he absorbed everything—books and magazines on golf course maintenance, bird watching, and Montessori schools, for example—and he related the knowledge he gained in ways that could enhance his projects. Intellectual curiosity seemed to energize him and infect others. "I find myself, up to this day, afraid not to read something because I think I might miss something," says Rummell.

James J. Chaffin, Jr., chairman of Chaffin/Light Associates in Spring Island, South Carolina, spent his early career years working for Fraser. "Most folks who encountered Charles would describe him as a brilliant visionary, constantly on the edge, and impatient with small thoughts," says Chaffin. "Brilliant, yes. Visionary, yes. Impatient, yes. But, what I remember most was his courage, persistence, and tenacity during the most difficult of times. Those traits have been an inspiration that I have called on during challenging times."

Sea Pines had its own internal market research department with 11 employees. Diana Permar, president of Permar, Inc., a market research firm in Charleston, South Carolina, was one of them. "Charles had an unbelievable curiosity about things," she says. "He appreciated the value of research and made links [to information] in ways that you couldn't have expected. Charles was unlike any other CEO I had been around. He asked so many questions. As a researcher, you couldn't out research him. He just read so much."

Research, according to Permar, was never predictable or linear for Fraser. It was part of his creative process. He didn't predetermine what data he would need; he simply collected all the information he could and then let the chips fall where they may. True to his nature, he shared what he learned with others. Says Mozley: "There never has been a file that I didn't have on top of my desk that had CEF on it, for Charles E. Fraser, because every month I got something from him. He was very well-read and inspired that in others."

**"He was just an incredible student of human nature and behavior. He made his communities rich based on the ideas he absorbed about what people liked and what they wanted."**

# Charles Fraser

## BIOGRAPHY

As a young boy growing up in rural Hinesville, Georgia, Charles Fraser's head was always buried in a book. Reared by well-educated parents—a former schoolteacher and an Army general—he was a budding thinker even back then. As a result, it comes as no surprise that he later saw in Hilton Head a wealth of potential, a stunning sea island that could be molded into an innovative recreational and residential oasis.

Fraser had an amazing ability to draw connections between seemingly unrelated things. According to Michael Danielson, author of *Profits and Politics in Paradise: The Development of Hilton Head Island*, after attending Presbyterian College and the University of Georgia, Fraser spent a summer on Hilton Head before leaving for Yale Law School. While at Yale, "his thoughts kept returning to Hilton Head, and his choice of studies was shaped by his growing sense of the potential of the holdings of his father's company on the island. Pursuing his interest, Fraser studied design and planning as well as law."

**Fraser (second from right) saw "the opportunity of a lifetime" in Hilton Head.**

*Courtesy of the Fraser family*

Fraser's father held a substantial interest in timber and miles and miles of land. When Fraser took a course at Yale, "Land Use Planning and Allocation by Private Agreement," it triggered a whirlwind of possibilities in his mind about the use of covenants and how they could be applied to invoke comprehensive land use planning.

His father's support and financial resources were critical to the 26-year-old's success. But as Danielson observed, Fraser also had the wherewithal "to translate vision into reality because of his skill, creativity, leadership, and hard work." Thus began an incredible journey in which Fraser eventually came to control nearly 5,000 acres, or more than seven square miles, on Hilton Head.

In addition to setting up the Hilton Head Company and Sea Pines Company, he established the Charles E. Fraser Company, a provider of planning services to developers worldwide. As a consultant, Fraser was instrumental coming up with a barrage of ideas for Walt Disney's new town of Celebration.

His unfettered thinking was often way ahead of the crowd—sometimes to a fault. Fraser's protégés recall he was occasionally guilty of going off on a tangent. But, to him, there was always a lesson to be learned, even if extravagantly taught.

For example, Fraser believed most companies suffered from what he called "not invented here," or NIH. Because they did not originate an idea themselves, they felt they could not use it. Fraser thought differently.

It was not unusual for him to charter two airplanes and take his employees around the United States to tour other resorts. As many as 100 people would take those trips, affectionately dubbed "Sea Pines University," even when Fraser did not have enough money to pay for them.

For years, according to Harry Frampton, Fraser would also regularly take his boat out of Harbortown and invite one or two employees to join the trip. During the week, he would also scout for other interesting guests to invite. His sole purpose was to generate great dialogue and pick peoples' brains about new trends. He would ask a doctor about medicine, or an architect to share what was going on in New York City. The boat would sit in the middle of Calibogue Sound for hours as the party talked and exchanged ideas.

"He was just an incredible student of human nature and behavior," says Michael Ainslie. "He made his communities rich based on the ideas he absorbed about what people liked and what they wanted."

In December 2002, Fraser died at age 73 in a boating accident. At the time, South Carolina governor Mark Sanford summed up the feelings of many when he said, "Our world and our state would be a better place if more people focused on the world of ideas the way Charles did."

CHAPTER THREE

# JAMES GRAASKAMP:
## Reinventing Real Estate Education

Desiree French

### LEADERSHIP LESSON
**Search for opportunities by seeking innovative ways to change, grow, and improve.**

"When people talk about their personal best leadership experiences, they talk about the challenge of change. When we look at leaders, we see that they're associated with transformations, whether small or large. Leaders don't have to change history, but they do have to make a change in 'business as usual.'"

*The Leadership Challenge*—James M. Kouzes and Barry Z. Posner

James Graaskamp, an eloquent and mesmerizing man, did not set out to change the world. He simply wanted to turn it upside down—at least as it pertained to real estate.

In the 1960s and 1970s, Graaskamp was consumed by an overwhelming desire to elevate real estate to a legitimate and distinct plane within academia, which he did. The gifted professor set a high standard for excellence in real estate education that, to this day, still distinguishes him as the leading scholar in real estate more than 16 years after his death.

"He created a vision of real estate education that did not exist before. He sort of put it all together," says Roderick Matthews, a senior lecturer in the Department of Real Estate and Urban Land Economics at the University of Wisconsin–Madison (UW–Madison), where Graaskamp taught for more than two decades. "I think he really created the modern real estate education curriculum, and he did it in a way that motivated everyone who knew him."

**"His legacy was applying the rigorous thinking of academia to work out meaningful real-life problems. His genius was keeping the two together."**

His enthusiasm was infectious. Whether lecturing to loyal students—who affectionately called him "The Chief"—industry practitioners at ULI seminars, or professionals overseas, he displayed a great passion for real estate and a vast reservoir of knowledge that few possess.

Graaskamp's theories about land appraisal and planning cemented his reputation among colleagues. And his rigorous and comprehensive curriculum was responsible for UW–Madison's consistent ranking as one of the top real estate schools nationally. UW–Madison was widely hailed as "the West Point of real estate."

Under Graaskamp's tutelage, the school's program emphasized a practical approach to real estate education and was the first in the nation to specialize in development analysis using computers.

"His legacy was applying the rigorous thinking of academia to work out meaningful real-life problems," says Mike Miles, a managing principal with Guggenheim Partners Real Estate in New York, who once

**Graaskamp viewed real estate as a multidisciplinary field.**

*The University of Wisconsin*

worked under Graaskamp. "His genius was keeping the two together."

Graaskamp was also instrumental in influencing a whole generation of real estate professionals—namely, his students, and there were hundreds of them. They were his life. He was completely and eternally devoted to them, and vice versa. Once they moved on and found jobs, which he routinely helped them get, the ties that bound them to their former professor endured.

An incredible number of alumni from the UW–Madison program went on to achieve an impressive array of success as entrepreneurs or chief executive officers of real estate companies. In fact, they competed with Ivy Leaguers for the top jobs throughout the industry.

Graaskamp had prepared them well. Their credentials and discipline were immaculate. He had instilled in them a strong work ethic and had provided the necessary tools they needed to compete. In cities such as Minneapolis and Chicago, the close-knit group of graduates was dubbed by some as the "Wisconsin Mafia."

"We had to be in labs at night and on the weekends to work on projects that took an insane amount of time. When I finally went to work," says Dick Schaller, a UW–Madison graduate and the chief investment officer of CMD Realty Investors in Chicago, "I felt like I was on vacation. I should have gone to medical school."

Although he was popular with students, Graaskamp's style did not always sit well with his colleagues at the university. He was too unconventional, outspoken, and critical of their theoretical approach to real estate. Graaskamp championed creative problem solving and saw real estate as more than merely a set of relationships between buyers and sellers. Rather, he viewed it as a multi-disciplinary field.

Joni Brooks, a partner with Duvernay + Brooks in New York, a consultant to public and private sector developers of affordable housing and a development partner on urban revitalization and affordable housing development, studied under Graaskamp in the 1970s. "He was forceful, brilliant, and just sort of took on the establishment," she says.

But, more important, "He taught you how to think. He demanded that you think out of the box," says Brooks. "I think I'm attracted to new, innovative ideas and I'm not fearful of them because he taught me how to break them into components and use analytical skills to approach them."

When it came to the big picture, Graaskamp was certainly a generalist. He taught the basics of appraisal and development, but he also managed to incorporate statistics, communication, and marketing into the UW–Madison curriculum. To get a comprehensive real estate education, he felt that students needed to grasp such topics as ethics, law, business, land use, and public policy. His goal was to have them do real estate well, which entailed mastering all the components that were vital to the whole.

> **"We had to be in labs at night and on the weekends to work on projects that took an insane amount of time. When I finally went to work, I felt like I was on vacation. I should have gone to medical school."**

**Graaskamp demanded that his students "think outside the box."**

*The University of Wisconsin*

During his tenure, Graaskamp also operated his own consulting firm, Landmark Research, Inc., which enabled him to personally tie academia with the real world. Besides being an adviser to bankers, land developers, and insurance companies, he was the cofounder of a general

**Graaskamp instilled an "uncommon" personal and professional ethic in his students.**

*The University of Wisconsin*

contracting firm, a land development company, and a farm investment corporation.

"Graaskamp was one of those people who had no peers. He was just brilliant, but he also had a soul," says former student Schaller. "He saw real estate as more than a means to produce a profit. He saw it as integral to shaping lives."

In Graaskamp's mind, those in the real estate profession were charged with a huge responsibility. They were stewards who formed a partnership between the user group and the government. He often said that every successful project provides dividends to the community at large—and if it did not, it was not successful.

"I believe that he instilled an ethic in people. If you go out into the real world and look at the people he affected, you will find a personal and professional ethic that is uncommon," says former student Mike Arneson, president of TOLD Development Company in Milwaukee. "I think that's his true legacy."

Although Graaskamp was a nationally recognized expert in real estate appraisal and had an extensive background in risk management and insurance, many believe that his major contribution was motivating his students and encouraging them to have careers in real estate. He never tired of teaching his young charges. In fact, while most professors taught one or two classes, Graaskamp taught four or five.

"His whole approach was a Jesuit approach, a Socratic approach," says Jim Curtis, a principal in the Bristol Group, a real estate investment and development firm in San Francisco. Curtis, who once studied under Graaskamp, now requires everyone who works for him to read two Graaskamp papers, "A Rational Approach to Feasibility Analysis" and "The Real Estate Process."

What most impressed Curtis is that "Graaskamp probably took more C students and turned them into overperformers than anyone I knew in my life. He always said attitude and passion are more important than anything else. He would even fight with the dean to get average students in that he thought could make a difference."

**"He was just brilliant, but he also had a soul. He saw real estate as more than a means to produce a profit. He saw it as integral to shaping lives."**

According to Rachelle Levitt, executive vice president of policy and practice for the Urban Land Institute, Graaskamp strongly influenced ULI's real estate education program. "His influence is still evident today," Levitt says. "ULI's real estate school and books have roots with Graaskamp. He challenged ULI to think about the next generations."

# James Graaskamp

## BIOGRAPHY

Even sitting in a wheelchair, it was obvious that James Graaskamp was a big, towering fellow. He was about 6'6" tall and weighed nearly 300 pounds. A gifted academic, he possessed a vast intellect and a razor-sharp wit. He indulged in deep-sea fishing, blues music, and his students. To know him was to love him, or to hate him. Some say there was no middle ground.

"He was a tough guy. Even though he was a quadriplegic, you didn't have to cut him any slack," according to Mike Miles, who worked under Graaskamp for one year in the Department of Real Estate and Urban Land Economics at the University of Wisconsin–Madison.

Before his death in 1988, Graaskamp was confined to a motorized wheelchair for 37 years. He was the victim of polio, which struck when he was a 17-year-old high school student in Milwaukee. Prior to contracting the disease, he had been awarded a football scholarship by Harvard University.

**Graaskamp insisted on making real estate education applicable to the real world.**

*The University of Wisconsin*

Rather than sulk, withdraw, and give in to his physical predicament, Graaskamp shrugged it off. He later referred to it as a "materials-handling problem." Unable to use his hands to write or type, he kept everything in his head—except a specially designed fishing rod, which he kept in his teeth.

"Within five minutes of being around him, you forgot he was in a wheelchair. He was captivating. He was the greatest raconteur that ever existed," says Jim Curtis, a former Graaskamp student and a principal in the Bristol Group real estate investment and development firm.

Graaskamp earned a bachelor's degree in creative writing from Rollins College, a master's in security analysis from Marquette University, and a doctorate in urban land economics and risk management from UW–Madison.

He joined the faculty of UW–Madison's School of Business Real Estate in 1964 and became chairman of the real estate department four years later. Thus began his long-term love affair with teaching students, whom he groomed to assume some of the most prestigious jobs in real estate and other industries.

Graaskamp literally served them to the end. He died on a Friday, but reportedly was in his office the previous Wednesday after having suffered considerable pain from a recent fall that broke his hip. Despite his condition, he visited with a long line of students who sought his help in getting summer jobs. Not until the line was finished and every single student was helped did he go to the hospital.

"It was typical of how he interacted with students," says Roderick Matthews, a senior lecturer in the real estate department.

Not as pleasant was his interaction with other scholars. He liked to challenge the academic elite, somewhat critically, mainly because he felt they failed to make real estate applicable in the real world.

"He had the intellectual ability to take on any person, and he loved to do it, particularly with people who were theoretical and not practical," says Mike Arneson, who was one of Graaskamp's teaching assistants and is now a president of TOLD Development Company in Milwaukee.

Graaskamp's disability did not prevent him from traveling. At the invitations of former students, he took trips to Australia, Asia, and to cities throughout the United States. Once, in Hawaii, he insisted on going scuba diving. His personal assistants got him up on a gurney, and passersby thought they were trying to kill him.

Fanatical about deep-sea fishing, he traveled to places both near and far, including the wilds of Alaska, to indulge his pastime. Paralyzed from the neck down, Graaskamp was able to move his fingers a few inches, and while holding a stick in his teeth, would hit a series of switches on his rod when it was time to reel in the catch. All the fish went back to Wisconsin, where he would hold a fish fry for his students.

"Most people wouldn't consider doing most of the things he did," says Craig Manske, a former student and personal assistant to Graaskamp and now president of Development Solutions, a general contracting, real estate development, and investment firm in Chicago. "If there was a solution to a problem, he would find it. He never viewed himself as a handicapped person."

# CHAPTER FOUR

# GERALD D. HINES:
## Creating the Culture

Mike Sheridan

### LEADERSHIP LESSON
### Build trust.

"Leaders who balance ambition with competency
and integrity understand that building trust is their
main objective. For trust to take hold, the first thing
a leader must do is generate shared values, goals, visions,
or objectives with those she wishes to lead. The trust
factor is critical. As trust builds, exemplary leaders
also reward dissent. They encourage it. They
understand that, even if they momentarily experience
discomfort as a result of being told they are wrong, this
feeling is more than offset as trust increases, and dissenting
information makes better, more informed decisions."

*Learning to Lead*—Warren Bennis and Joan Goldsmith

Perhaps more than any other developer in the past century, Gerald D. Hines has influenced the skylines of some of North America's busiest cities. Hines' projects are as bold a statement about architecture as they are about successful real estate development—the trapezoidal towers of Pennzoil Place in Houston, the cylindrical 101 California Street in San Francisco, and the elliptical elegance of the "Lipstick Building" on 53rd at Third in Manhattan.

Such structures are great accomplishments to be sure, but Hines believes that perhaps one of his greatest achievements—and possibly one of his best assets—is people. To Hines, success is derived from creating an environment in which people are what matter most, quality counts, and innovation is celebrated. For nearly half a century, Hines has attracted, hired, trained, and mentored professionals who exemplify—and are justifiably proud of—the company.

**". . . it's not the policies, procedures, or programs that have made the difference at Hines. It's been the people."**

Tom Kruggel, vice president of operations for Hines's West Regional Office in San Francisco, says the Hines concept is simple: It's not about building the biggest office tower, not about towering egos, and not about accumulating wealth. It's all about the 2,800 professionals at Hines. "It's a pretty simple concept," Kruggel says. "There are a lot of excellent programs and procedures out there, many of which Hines developed. But it's not the policies, procedures, or programs that have made the difference at Hines. It's been the people."

That is a testament to the way Gerald D. Hines built his business: creatively, carefully, and with a dedicated core of executives whose loyalty is steadfast after many years. Hines not only identified, recruited, and retained some of the most talented people in development, but he also changed the face of many cities by providing, through his developments, a better place for the cities' residents to live, work, or both.

"What's fascinating to me is that many of the people Gerry trained, for the most part, are still here," says Hines executive vice president

**Hines's "Lipstick Building" at 53rd and Third streets in Manhattan offers an elliptical elegance.**

*Hines*

Louis Sklar, who joined the firm 36 years ago. "Gerry didn't just create a development company, he built a family of talented individuals who have chosen to stay at Hines and who continue to form the core of our organization."

Jeff Hines, the company's chief executive officer and Gerald's son, says his dad set out to create a corporate culture that attracted the best and the brightest—and retained them. "There is a strong culture that comes with having worked a long time at Hines," he says. "Strategically, it is very important for people to make their careers here. We have a strong bias toward organic growth, which creates a group outlook and allows us to be international in scope, while at the same time to feel comfortable about decentralized decision making. People who have grown up with the firm know how Dad approaches the business—with integrity, creativity, and a constant awareness of our highly prized reputation."

Over the years, Hines has developed a culture in which not only is the entrepreneurial spirit celebrated, but creativity—the innate ability to develop new ways of doing old things—is prized. Within the Hines organization, good ideas are revered and individuals who share new strategies and develop best practices are rewarded. Employees are encouraged to make educated decisions, effect change, and set in motion innovative strategies and solutions. It goes without saying that at any high-powered organization, most of the professionals are hard working. But at Hines, employees are also curious, constantly seeking new challenges, and aching to create projects in which they can take enormous pride.

According to the elder Hines, part of his company's success is based on its ability to be both a local and an international company, serving specific market needs in many corners of the world. Although the company's central headquarters remains in Houston, it has 17 regional offices, including 11 that cover foreign markets; within each region are multiple offices. "One of the strengths of our organization is our regional capability, in which we act as a local developer, yet we are an international developer," Hines says. The regional structure, which was somewhat unusual in the industry when Hines initiated it years ago, is a "constantly evolving" operation involving shifts in authority between the headquarters and regional offices, Hines explains.

**"Gerry didn't just create a development company, he built a family of talented individuals who have chosen to stay at Hines and who continue to form the core of our organization."**

The firm is privately held; Gerald and Jeff Hines own it. However, the senior management participates in the profits and losses. With an average tenure of more than 25 years, the executive team members have a well-established stake in the company's course. "The most important aspect of building this company was to get outstanding leaders and let them participate. They are with us for the long term, not a job-hopping opportunity," Hines says.

"As we get more far-flung in terms of operations, it's important that our people in those regions are making decisions within a construct that is consistent with how we would act if we [the central office] were there," Jeff Hines says. "Our reputation is our all-important asset, and we feel it's going to be a rare circumstance where we have to worry about someone doing something from an integrity perspective that will wind up being a hit to our reputation."

John Harris, executive vice president at Hines, has been intimately involved in many of the more than 500 projects built by the firm. He joined Hines in 1966, and from the start was encouraged to think creatively. "One of the things Gerry did and taught the rest of us to do was to have a productive and respectful dialogue with others, especially world-class designers, that leads to an appropriate compromise," Harris says. "A dialogue doesn't have to be a battle of egos. Each side has to understand the other's position. That's one of the biggest parts of our success—our people know how to do that. Gerry has a real passion for architecture. But he also has the ability to teach other people the process to obtain that good architecture. Not a lot of developers have the talent to do it themselves, and then pass along their passion and knowledge for others to do the same."

Hines gave company associates such as Harris the freedom to bring striking design to cities at what he considered an appropriate cost. Jeff Hines explains, "Dad excelled at creating great architecture at a commercially reasonable price in a manner that created terrific space for tenants. He pursued the best design, the best architects, and the best people. There was a lot of creative tension, a lot of discussion between us and the architect about the drawings all the way from the conceptual stage through the whole drawing process. It was a push–pull process. But it was always one of mutual respect. That's part of our culture."

Early on, Hines set out to build landmarks—structures that not only caught the eye and stirred the imagination, but also lured people inside. He grasped that excellent design can boost a project's bottom line and enhance a building's value to tenants and the community. In nearly any major city in the United States, some of the most prestigious office projects are likely to be Hines developments. Many of them are designed by well-known architects: I. M. Pei, Philip Johnson, Cesar Pelli, Frank Gehry, and Robert A.M. Stern, to name a few.

Hines's deep appreciation of architecture and his keen eye for design have been handed down to his employees. Cutting-edge creations and aesthetics have always been the basis for his company's reputation. But the beauty of a Hines building is more than just skin deep. Hines is always willing to take the risk of innovation. He instinctively seeks that "point of difference" in a design—that special something that makes a building stand out.

"When I first started, Gerry was building on Richmond Avenue in Houston, and what's interesting is that most of those buildings can still be identified as Hines buildings," Sklar says. "Even back then, Gerry sought good architecture and had a very heavy involvement in all components of the project. He challenged the experts over and over again. He'd ask 'Do you really need this, does it have to be that way?' He wanted good architecture, but he added market considerations to the equations. And he always was respectful of others' opinions."

Respecting and nurturing has always been a key to Hines's success. "I think it is attention to detail that helped make us successful. We looked at every single item," Sklar continues. "We'd go over the façade, we'd examine the curtain wall, we'd look at the elevators, the HVAC [heating, ventilation, and air conditioning], the plumbing, the electrical—everything. Our people still do."

**"Hines and his staff strongly believe that architecture has a positive effect on quality of life. . . . He has been a role model not only for the industry, but for his own company as well."**

Hines's projects strive to combine beauty with functionality—many can be described as innovative, yet invitingly familiar and practical; daring, yet appropriate. "High-quality architecture does not mean that you throw away the budget. It means that you design the best product within that budget," Hines says. "You must adhere to certain disciplines or it is not a repeatable processs. A repeatable process is one that is economically successful, not necessarily in the architecture, but in the process. We've done low-cost warehouses, but with a little flair, a little something extra. Not all of our buildings are going to win an AIA [American Institute of Architects] award, but they will all be very good citizens in their community."

**A fountain at Hines's Diagonal Mar Community in Barcelona, Spain.**

*Hines*

According to Paul Goldberger, architecture critic of the *New Yorker* magazine, Gerald Hines demonstrated that not only could a real estate developer produce good architecture at an acceptable cost, but also that doing so would add value and create demand. "Hines saw greater sophistication in the world and increasing willingness to pay more for a better product," says Goldberger, who is also dean of the Parsons School of Design at New School University in New York City. "We look now at buildings not only in commercial terms, but in emotional and image terms. Well-designed buildings have become civic symbols."

Equally important, Goldberger notes, is that Hines passed on his passion for great architecture throughout the ranks of the Hines organization. "Hines and his staff strongly believe that architecture has a positive effect on quality of life, and that architecture has become a factor in society," he says. "He has been a role model not only for the industry, but for his own company as well."

The commitment Hines has made to high-quality construction and good practices in architecture, building materials, sustainability, and business operations earned him the 2002 Urban Land Institute J.C. Nichols Prize for Visionaries in Urban Development. The prize, named for legendary Kansas City, Missouri, developer Jesse Clyde Nichols, recognizes an individual whose career demonstrates a commitment to the highest standards of responsible development.

According to Joseph E. Brown, president and chief executive officer of EDAW, Inc., in San Francisco, and a member of the 2002 Nichols

Prize jury, Hines's desire to contribute to a better urban environment—not just produce a better building—exemplified the ideals of the prize. "Gerry builds communities with a sense that they will be here forever. He's never doing it for the short run," Brown says.

Few would argue that when most people think of Gerald D. Hines, they think of beautiful communities. But when asked how he wants to be remembered, this industry leader does not hesitate to put people first. "Professionally, I want to be remembered for the quality and integrity of our organization and our work," he says.

# Gerald D. Hines

## BIOGRAPHY

Four years ago, to celebrate turning 75, fitness enthusiast Gerald Hines donned his in-line skates and took off up a mountain outside of Aspen, Colorado, where he owns a vacation home and spends part of each year.

There are far flatter pedestrian trails that weave throughout the town—certainly enough for a sufficient workout. But sticking to those would have been too easy. Hines does not like to do just enough; he prefers to excel and challenge himself in the process. And that is the approach he has used in building the Hines firm from a single-room, office warehouse construction company into a multibillion-dollar, multifaceted real estate organization with offices worldwide.

Born in Gary, Indiana, he spent part of his youth selling shoes in a department store, and has joked that he got into development "because I knew I did not want to sell shoes for a living." He graduated from Purdue University with a degree in mechanical engineering, and built warehouses on the side for several years before founding Hines in 1957. His first skyscraper, the 50-story One Shell Plaza in Houston, designed by Skidmore, Owings & Merrill and completed in 1971, was the first of

**Gerald (right) and
Jeff Hines.**

*Hines*

many subsequent projects to "give me knots in my stomach," he says with a chuckle.

From the outset, Hines maintained that rather than sacrificing beauty for profit, beauty could be used to enhance it. "I was intrigued with trying to achieve outstanding architecture in office warehouses. We evolved a way to work with an architect and produce a building in an economical way, and we got a lot of business because of our architecture," he says.

Hines's background as an engineer instilled in him a penchant for details, which has contributed to the success of his buildings, says Peter Rummell, chairman and chief executive officer of the St. Joe Company in Jacksonville, Florida. "Gerry has a detailed view of the world, as well as a global view, and good design comes from paying a lot of attention to details. You have to start with a vision that goes beyond what you are working on, but then you have to execute against that vision, and the execution is in the details," Rummell says. "That's not something you phone in. It's something you spend a lot of hours poring over, and putting yourself in the consumer's position of how that project will be experienced. Some people know how to do this. Others don't. Gerry does."

Hines, who lives part-time in London, now spends much of his time overseeing the company's European operations, while his son, Jeff Hines, runs Hines's U.S. headquarters and oversees activities in Asia and Latin America. For the elder Hines, relinquishing day-to-day control of the entire operation was made easier given the experience and loyalty of its top management.

As the years have passed, being able to trust others with the company has allowed Gerald Hines more free time to pursue his personal interests—skating, skiing, cycling, tennis, and enjoying his family. "You always regret that you did not spend more time with your family. But I think I've maintained a reasonable balance between work and family, and I look forward to many years of being with my family," he says.

Hines has never had second thoughts about entering the development profession, and he believes some of the industry's best work is yet to come. "Development is a very exciting, imaginative field. It involves many disciplines and the interaction with so many parts of our world: finance, politics, people, science, psychology. It's got to be one of the most interesting occupations, because it touches the lives of so many people," he says. "We [those in the development community] are on our way to better-quality development. I am very optimistic about where we are headed," Hines says.

CHAPTER FIVE

# JAMES ROUSE: Leading from the Heart

Trisha Riggs

## LEADERSHIP LESSON
### Be yourself.

"We are all drawn to authentic leaders. We admire them, count on them, and wonder what mysterious quality attracts us to them. Yet their secret is easy to discover: They are clear about who they are. To become leaders in our work lives, each of us needs to develop our capacity for authenticity. Only when we wake up to ourselves and act with integrity can we begin to ask the same of others. Authentic leaders know what they want, why they want it, and how to communicate what they want to others to gain their cooperation and support for achieving their goals."

*Learning to Lead*—Warren Bennis and Joan Goldsmith

Those who knew the late James Rouse describe him as a great communicator. His passion, enthusiasm, and optimism were contagious and inspired confidence.

"He could talk people into doing things they never thought they'd do when they started," says Jeffrey Donahue, a 30-year Rouse Company employee, who now heads Rouse's Enterprise Social Investment Corporation, which raises funds for affordable housing projects nationwide.

Coupled with his ability to communicate and motivate, Rouse was a risk taker, which led him from mortgage banking into developing shopping centers in the mid-1950s.

Rouse understood the value of great architectural design and land use planning. He tempered this with the belief that development should be people-oriented. Although his vision of integrating public gathering places into project design seems commonplace today, it was revolutionary in the late 1950s.

**"He demonstrated a personal commitment that spoke volumes. Jim was more than just philanthropic; he wasn't simply throwing money at the problem—he was personally involved."**

Immediately following the development of his first shopping mall in Baltimore, Rouse turned his attention to urban renewal with projects in Baltimore and in southwest Washington. In keeping with his civic spirit, he also organized the Greater Baltimore Committee in 1955 to spur downtown urban revitalization. Although it may have appeared a dichotomy at the time, Rouse believed that he could simultaneously improve both suburbs and downtowns.

According to former Baltimore Mayor Kurt Schmoke, Rouse had a history of civic activism, particularly in efforts to improve Baltimore's worst neighborhoods. "He demonstrated a personal commitment that spoke volumes. Jim was more than just philanthropic; he wasn't simply throwing money at the problem—he was personally involved," Schmoke said.

**Rouse (left) at the opening of Baltimore's Harborplace in 1980.**

*The Rouse Corporation*

Rouse was ever the trendsetter who created value with his projects, according to Mathias (Matt) DeVito, Rouse's successor as chairman of The Rouse Company. "He had this outlook that nothing was impossible," DeVito recalls.

In the 1960s, Rouse applied his skills as a visionary to the creation of a new town—Columbia, Maryland—to be situated halfway between Washington, D.C., and Baltimore, talking then-chair of Connecticut General, Frasier Wilde, into financing the venture.

"Before he built Columbia, he established a faculty of sociologists, urban planners, educators, philosophers, all sorts of people to think out what a congenial community involved—even to the point of saying that there ought to be a disruptive factor in every community—that you needed somebody to stir things up," says Charles "Mac" Mathias, former U.S. Senator and longtime Rouse friend. "There was nothing that escaped him; he paid a great deal of attention to details."

By all accounts, Rouse was a magnet for attracting people of quality. Donahue of the Enterprise Social Investment Corporation was recruited by the Rouse Company in 1973 while attending the Wharton School of Business. Rouse "set a standard of the life you ought to lead," says Donahue.

DeVito was a partner with Piper Marbury, and the Rouse Company was his account. He left the firm in 1968 and signed on with Rouse as general counsel. "It was like a partnership, we went through a lot together and the company became successful. It was a very close relationship that caused me to stay," says DeVito. In 1973, Rouse handed his company over to DeVito to manage.

"Jim created the Rouse Company and I think that Matt saved the Rouse Company," says Donahue. "DeVito took the company that had grown very rapidly and brought the classical textbook next stage of business practices, which it needed."

"There's nobody else in the field who's like James Rouse, who started as a mortgage banker, got involved in regional shopping centers, and then moved on to Columbia," says Robert E. Simon, the founder of the planned town of Reston, Virginia. "And after that, he did his most important work, which was in trying to move our country in the direction of affordable housing."

Although Rouse was steadfastly committed to all his pursuits, perhaps his greatest passion was the Enterprise Foundation, which he established in 1980 at the age of 66 after retiring from the Rouse Company. To date, the foundation has provided $4.4 billion in equity loans and grants to 2,400 housing nonprofits, leading to the construction of more than 150,000 homes for low-income families in 860 communities nationwide.

Its work hooked Bart Harvey, who initially viewed his stint at Enterprise as temporary. Harvey joined the foundation in 1984 on a six-month sabbatical from a Wall Street investment banking firm; 20 years later, Harvey is the organization's chairman and chief executive officer, carrying on the Rouse legacy as Rouse's hand-picked successor.

> **"You just watched what he did and the lives he touched and the difference that he made. He had tremendous joy and incredible vision as to what could happen."**

**Rouse (left) greets a resident of Columbia, Maryland.**

*The Rouse Corporation*

**Rouse works on a house for Habitat for Humanity International.**

*The Rouse Corporation*

"I think what was most amazing about Jim was he didn't preach. He was a terrific salesman, though, and he made sure I was following him around. You just watched what he did and the lives he touched and the difference that he made. It was like a constant revelation from just being around him. He had tremendous joy and incredible vision as to what could happen," Harvey says.

Rouse's philosophy started from the premise that business is to serve human needs, Harvey notes. "His point was that if you allow people's talents to blossom and grow, the bottom line of that is the bottom line—profit." He describes his former boss as "90 percent perspiration and 10 percent genius. . . .He would show you a different way of looking at something. I'm still not convinced that he wasn't crazy."

According to Donahue, if there is a Rouse company model, it is based on the belief that "It's not necessarily easy, but it is possible to have a company that is both socially responsible and profitable." While he concedes that it is not feasible for every business to be completely socially focused, the Rouse Company—through Rouse's leadership—has demonstrated that it is possible to "produce a good product for a decent price, support its employees well, encourage volunteerism, and be generous in giving. That's what Jim hoped for."

# James Rouse

## BIOGRAPHY

The youngest of five children, James Rouse was born in Easton, Maryland, on April 26, 1914. He lost both parents during his senior year of high school, and his family home subsequently fell into foreclosure. This event may have triggered his life-long passion for providing housing for those less fortunate.

His dream of attending Princeton was dashed, but his siblings provided a year at a preparatory school, and then he attended the University of Hawaii while living with an older sister and her husband, who served in the Navy. A scholarship took him to the University of Virginia, where he spent a year but dropped out because of limited finances. He headed to Baltimore in 1933 and pursued a law degree, parking cars to earn his living.

**"Produce a good product for a decent price, support its employees well, encourage volunteerism, and be generous in giving. . .that's what Jim hoped for."**

While attending law school at night, Rouse became assistant legal counsel at the newly established Federal Housing Administration in 1935, where he learned the basics of the building business. Although he earned his law degree and finished second on the state bar exam, he did not have an interest in becoming a lawyer.

Instead, Rouse saw an opportunity and sold the idea of a mortgage banking department to Title Guarantee. At age 22, he started the new mortgage department for the company. Realizing the chance for greater success, he formed a partnership with Hunter Moss in 1939 and set up an independent mortgage company. Their business was interrupted by World War II, but they hired someone to keep it going until their return from their war duties.

Rouse married Elizabeth Winstead in May 1941, and his military service was deferred until after the birth of their first child, Robin, in July 1942. Rouse served in the Navy and saw duty at Pearl Harbor working on a small, select staff for an admiral. In late 1944, he was reassigned to a command in Pensacola, Florida. He left military service a year later to return to Baltimore and get back to business.

With the end of the war came the beginning of the baby boom and the building boom. Rouse's business expanded, and he subsequently became active in the Mortgage Bankers Association and began testifying before Congress on housing issues.

Rouse's gift for public speaking and his concern for those less fortunate led him into the arena of urban redevelopment and political issues. In 1953, President Eisenhower appointed him chairman of an advisory committee on urban redevelopment. The committee's recommendations became part of the Housing Act of 1954.

Rouse's company became one of the foremost real estate development companies in the country.

His vision and risk-taking led to the development of shopping malls and festival marketplaces, and the creation of a new town called Columbia.

Rouse's 32-year marriage ended in 1973 and he met his second wife, Patty, several months later through mutual friends in Norfolk. They married in 1974 and lived in Columbia, where they both oversaw The Enterprise Foundation, which Rouse believed was his most important work.

President Bill Clinton awarded the Medal of Freedom to Rouse in September 1995, six months before his death on April 9, 1996, of Lou Gehrig's disease.

EXCERPTS FROM
*BETTER PLACES, BETTER LIVES:*
*A BIOGRAPHY OF JAMES ROUSE*
by Joshua Olsen
Published by the Urban Land Institute

On the morning of October 29, 1963, Rouse drove his station wagon up to where the courthouse in Ellicott City was perched, overlooking a narrow valley containing the town's 800 citizens and the muddy Patapsco River. He, in his rumpled tweed jacket, his brother, and a couple of key employees got out and walked across the lawn past one of Maryland's ubiquitous Confederate monuments, up the gray stairs, past a vending machine, and into a public meeting of the Howard County Commissioners.

At the appropriate moment, Rouse stepped forward and revealed that it was he, a shopping center developer from Baltimore, who now controlled 14,000 acres in the center of their county. But beyond finally removing the shroud from the land grab, he did not have many substantive details to give, and so merely remarked, "It will be our purpose, working closely with local officials and agencies, to plan a community that will fit naturally into the Howard County landscape, preserving the stream valleys, creating lakes and pools, protecting hills and forests, and providing recreation areas, parks, and greenbelts that will separate and give identity, scale, and protection to the developed areas."

. . . .A little bit of Columbia exists in every new residential development that stresses the importance of community, and in every edge city that manages to combine sites of employment, dwelling, shopping, and recreation in a suburban setting. . . .Rouse was no huckster.

CHAPTER SIX

# STEPHEN B. SIEGEL:
## Listening and Learning

Mike Sheridan

### LEADERSHIP LESSON
### Understand the ultimate power of relationships.

"First, you cannot teach talent. You cannot teach someone to form strong opinions, to feel the emotions of others, to revel in confrontations, or to pick up on the subtle differences in how best to manage each person. You have to select for talents like these.

Second, talents like these prove to be the driving force behind an individual's job performance. It's not that experience, brainpower, and willpower are unimportant. It's just that an employee's full complement of talents—what drives her, how she thinks, how she builds relationships—is more important."

*First, Break All the Rules*—Marcus Buckingham and Curt Coffman

Stephen B. Siegel was thrust into the rough and tumble New York City real estate world at the innocent age of 17, serving as credit and collections manager for buildings managed by the national realty firm of Cushman & Wakefield. There was no better way to cut your teeth in the industry, Siegel later recalled, than learning rejection first-hand. "I'd introduce myself and say, 'Hello, I've come for your rent. You're about a month past due,'" said Siegel. "They'd say 'Shut up and get out of here.' It was a great training ground. You learned to develop your people skills very quickly."

Siegel didn't dwell on the rejections. Instead he sought to develop a rapport with the lessees. By engaging the tenants—asking about their family's health, how their business was doing and so forth—he soon was able to collect the back rents and move up the corporate ladder. Two decades later, he was named president and chief executive of Cushman & Wakefield, later leaving for a stint in the development business with the Chubb Corporation. He was on his way to sales superstardom.

> "His people skills are legendary. He'll see someone ten years later and still recall details instantly. That makes a very, very strong connection and the ability to make that strong connection with people makes him a very good leader."

In the early 1990s, he joined the Edward S. Gordon Company (ESG), working alongside real estate legend Edward Gordon. When ESG merged with Insignia, Siegel was named chairman and CEO of Insignia/ESG. Two years ago, when Insignia/ESG combined with CB Richard Ellis (CBRE), Siegel became chairman of global brokerage, responsible for advising major corporations and property owners around the globe on a wide range of real estate issues.

Although his professional achievements are exceptional, what most colleagues and clients praise about Siegel is his leadership style—listening closely to what people are saying, willing to publicly admit he doesn't know everything, and cultivating individual talent within the organization. His mastery of making people feel immediately at ease, his

**Stephen Siegel (third from right) with Cushman & Wakefield colleagues at a New Jersey office in 1979.**

*CBRE*

phenomenal memory for details, and his ability to talk to an individual and make that person feel they are the most important human being in the room have served him well in his decades-long real estate career.

"What makes Steve different from 95 percent of other real estate professionals I have worked with is that he is one of the most engaging, people-oriented executives I know," says Tony LoPinto, managing director and chief executive of Equinox, a real estate executive search firm. "What distinguishes Steve from the pack are his managerial and people skills. Most of the people he has dealt with over the years don't just consider him a competitor or even a boss. They consider him a friend."

Siegel's management style is one of personal engagement, LoPinto added. "Real estate can be a pretty cut-throat business and Steve is hard-driving. He's shrewd. He's very entrepreneurial. But the people Steve deals with truly feel touched by him. He engages people on a personal level. That is a very powerful motivational tool."

Unlike a general who rarely meets the men and women he leads into battle, Siegel seeks to get to know his troops. He goes out of his way to foster a positive frame of mind among his staff, sometimes strolling around the office asking, "How's it going?"—a simple gesture that provides a quick lift. Ask a CBRE employee and they'll reveal the secret to Siegel's success: He listens. He motivates. He inspires. He leads with empathy and sensitivity.

"Steve is proof that nice guys can finish first," said Tom Bermingham, executive director of CBRE's brokerage division and Siegel's former working partner. "But don't get the wrong impression. He's also a fiery competitor who seeks to inspire. Steve is clearly a perfectionist who delights in getting the job done. His people skills are legendary. He has a wonderful memory. He'll see someone ten years later and still recall details instantly. That makes a very, very strong connection and the ability to make that strong connection with people makes him a very good leader."

**"You are never too old to learn, or to find a different way of doing things. As an executive, you need to surround yourself with some people who are smarter than you are."**

Siegel always listens intently to the person he is speaking with, continued Bermingham. "He's not looking over your shoulder to see who might be more important in the room. He gives his full attention to the person he is speaking with—no matter what their social status is."

To Siegel, communication is not only about getting the message across; it is about listening to hear whether the correct message was received. Most chief executives are often carried away by their own enthusiasm and lack the patience to listen to others. What makes Siegel different and ultimately more successful is that he recognizes that listening closely provides a source of additional information that can be used later on.

"A lot of people don't really listen; their mind is somewhere else," Siegel explained. "But I make an effort to concentrate when people talk with me. I really want to hear what they have to say because I want to act on it. In that way, I might be able anticipate minor problems before they become major ones. Listening carefully helps to keep the ship sailing smoothly. You also have to understand when to say no, and I've found the earlier you do that—if you have to—the better. People want to be dealt with honestly. They would rather have you say 'no' now than wait for weeks to get the same answer."

**Siegel (left) "knows how to deal with people and has a genuine interest in them."**

*The PhotoBureau, New York*

As important as listening is learning. Siegel places a heavy emphasis on "learning up"—gaining knowledge from others in the corporate ranks. It's the opposite from the approach taken at many firms, where training and information flow downhill from the chief executive officer. But Siegel seeks to ensure that knowledge flows upwards as well, to encourage innovation and competitiveness. He actively seeks data from the rank-and-file, recognizing that employees want to contribute their ideas and receive acknowledgment for their efforts.

"You can never assume you understand it all or are able to grasp everything there is to know about the business," explains Siegel. "You are never too old to learn, or to find a different way of doing things. As an executive, you need to surround yourself with some people who are smarter than you are. Jack Welch, the former chief executive of General Electric, had very smart people around him who later went on to become CEOs of major corporations. He wasn't afraid to learn. Knowledge, it is said, can be power."

Knowledge is becoming an increasingly valuable corporate asset. Insignia and CBRE merged not only for financial success, Siegel said, "but also because we wanted the increased intellectual capacity. We not only did financial due diligence on the deal, but we also performed human due diligence. We looked at the individual talent in the company and tried to figure out how we could nurture that collective intelligence to help grow the business."

While enjoying the business tremendously, Siegel is a strong believer in community involvement. The roster of his charitable contributions is almost as long as the list of his accomplishments in the real estate industry. "He is extremely generous with his time, serving on different boards and helping to raise money for various charitable organizations," said Bermingham. "It's for his personal satisfaction, not to make more contacts for business. It's heartfelt."

From Siegel's point of view, it's simply something that individuals do. "My mother, Ann, was a school crossing guard and my father, Charles, was a laborer," Siegel said. "I had one pair of pants for school. We were a lower-middle-class family. But my mother would sometimes bring home two or three kids she had met and give them lunch because she knew there were people worse off than we were. Things like that you don't forget, so when you become successful, you want to help as many others as you can."

By listening, learning, and leading, Steve Siegel has reached the pinnacle of real estate success. Throughout his career, he has focused on people rather than systems and structure and sought to inspire trust instead of exerting control. He leads rather than manages, and has mastered the art of attracting and motivating talented workers to achieve their potential.

> **"He continually works on his people skills and inspires his employees to achieve their greatest potential. He knows how to deal with people and has a genuine interest in them. It's something sought by nearly all leaders, but while all aspire to it, only a few like Steve Siegel achieve it."**

"Steve Siegel is a great leader because he engenders trust and confidence in all the people around him," said Jonathan Mechanic, chairman of the real estate group at the New York City law firm of Fried Frank Harris Shriver & Jacobson LLP. "He continually works on his people skills and inspires his employees to achieve their greatest potential. He knows how to deal with people and has a genuine interest in them. It's something sought by nearly all leaders, but while all aspire to it, only a few like Steve Siegel achieve it."

# Stephen B. Siegel

## BIOGRAPHY

Stephen B. Siegel's extensive experience spans more than four decades in the international real estate industry, the majority of those years serving as the top executive of three major real estate companies. He is widely regarded in commercial real estate circles as one of the real estate industry's most talented and prolific professionals.

Among a host of honors, he has been named by *Crain's Magazine* as one of the 100 most influential business leaders in New York City. Yet despite a heavy workload and a hectic travel schedule, he devotes a substantial amount of his time to charitable endeavors.

Siegel not only presides over one of the largest firms in the commercial real estate industry, but has dealt with some of the nation's most prominent corporate clients. During his brokerage career, Siegel arranged expansions and relocations of corporate headquarters for many corporations, law firms, and financial institutions, including: Simpson, Thacher & Bartlett; Arthur Young; Ebasco Services; Toys 'R' Us; Continental Insurance; and the Chubb Corporation. He also brokered the sale of such properties as 75 Rockefeller Center and 250 Park Avenue, and the acquisition of the land beneath Giants Stadium in the Meadowlands.

It's an impressive career for a New York youngster with a lot of ambition who started out in 1961 as a junior accountant at the well-known real estate firm of Cushman & Wakefield (C&W), where he worked for the next 27 years. Siegel rose through the C&W ranks—moving on to sales, and then opening the company's New Jersey office in 1981. A short time later, he became Cushman & Wakefield's president and chief executive officer, adding the title of chairman four years later.

But Siegel was restless. He left Cushman & Wakefield in 1988 to be president, chief executive officer, and principal of Chubb Realty, a new real estate development subsidiary of insurance leader Chubb Corporation. After 24 months, Siegel said he saw the industry shifting from a development-oriented business to a service-minded field. He then assumed the presidency of Edward S. Gordon Company (ESG), with real estate legend Ed Gordon retaining the chairmanship.

**Siegel (right) with Edward Gordon.**

At ESG, Siegel was involved in managing day-to-day operations as well as some tenant procurement, long-term planning, and broker recruitment. During a period of tremendous flux in the industry, Siegel correctly saw that much talent could be recruited to the ESG's team. On Siegel's watch, ESG's annual revenues surged from about $50 million to more than $700 million.

That performance caught the attention of other companies, and ESG later merged with Insignia to become Insignia/ESG. At Insignia/ESG, Siegel orchestrated a major national growth strategy that included the establishment of substantial brokerage operations in key central business districts across the country, the development of a national investment sales/financial services practice, and the expansion of the commercial property services portfolio.

His long involvement with charitable organizations includes service as the general chairman of the Association for the Help of Retarded Children; he was inducted into the association's Hall of Honor in 1999. He received honorary doctorate degrees from Monmouth University and Baruch College, was honored by the Crohns & Colitis Foundation with its "Man of the Year" Award, and has received New York University Real Estate Institute's Urban Leadership Award.

# CHAPTER SEVEN

# DONALD TERNER:
## Bridging the Gap in Low-Income Housing

Desiree French

## LEADERSHIP LESSON
### Be brave.

"You have to be brave to be a leader. . . .(E)very leader knows that no matter how well you plan, you may, at times, be faced with a completely unknown situation, or worse, a situation that make you unpopular in your decisions. That's the point where you're going to have to be brave. You'll come under fire, and, of course, you'll make certain that you're not sticking to your guns out of stubbornness, but rather, out of a conviction that you're right. . . ."

*Leadership for Dummies: A Reference for the Rest of Us—*
Marshall Loeb and Stephen Kindel

Before it became acceptable to voice concern about the dearth of affordable housing in America, Donald Terner was in the trenches championing the plight of the underdog, knocking down the walls of intolerance built by those who did not want low-cost housing in their backyards. By speaking up and rallying to make decent homes attainable for thousands of individuals and families, he made a tremendous difference in the affordable housing arena throughout America.

He exported his brand of relentless exuberance overseas to such places as Vietnam, South Africa, South America, and war-torn Bosnia. He became a national and international ambassador of goodwill, fighting on behalf of refugees, urban homesteaders, the homeless, and millions of working families locked out of the American Dream of homeownership.

As a pioneer and leader in the field of affordable housing, he preached self-help; wrote a book, *Freedom to Build*; and helped found two nonprofit housing organizations, the Urban Homesteading Assistance Board (UHAB) and BRIDGE Housing Corporation, which have called tremendous attention to the nation's shortage of affordable housing.

**"He could persuade anyone to do anything—city councilors, bankers, neighbors. It wasn't just good logic and the power of persuasion. He inspired people to do the right things, whether they were students, staffers, or private developers."**

While a professor at Harvard University and the Massachusetts Institute of Technology, and an associate dean of the University of California (UC) Berkeley College of Environmental Design, Terner also influenced a generation of students. Many of them have gone on to make lasting contributions working in government, nonprofit organizations, and the private sector on behalf of those seeking safe, clean, and affordable places to call home.

"He was very charismatic. He had a vision and a way of expressing it that was really inspiring," says Andrew Reicher, executive director of New York City–based UHAB. "He could talk corporate supporters and institutions out of anything. It wasn't just hype, because he delivered the vision he talked about. He knew how to take the world of business and apply business models, adapt them, or create new ones, in the nonprofit world. He knew how to get government, decision makers, and policy makers to act."

In fact, it was a Terner lecture at UC Berkeley in the 1970s on rebuilding communities and the formative work of UHAB that convinced Reicher to pursue a career in affordable housing. He even followed Terner into state government, serving as his special assistant when Terner was appointed by California governor Jerry Brown as the director of housing and community development.

**"Don was just a driving force, and he was tough. He wasn't a hands-off guy. Everything we do at BRIDGE today is guided by the principles of Don Terner."**

In that position, one of Terner's biggest accomplishments was pressing Caltrans, the California Department of Transportation, to set aside $300 million for affordable housing that was lost when the Century Freeway project was built in Los Angeles, displacing thousands of residents.

Rick Holliday, another former UC Berkeley student, also recalls stumbling into that same Terner lecture that so influenced Reicher. That class, Holliday says, completely reorganized his thinking about affordable housing and neighborhood revitalization.

Along with Terner, Holliday became a founding officer in the mid-1980s of BRIDGE Housing Corporation, a scrappy nonprofit development company in San Francisco that has become one of the nation's major builders of affordable housing, setting as its goal the construction of high-volume, high-quality homes. While there, the twosome, zealous about their mission, became known as "Batman and Robin."

"Don was the most influential person in my career," says Holliday, now president of Holliday Development Company in Emeryville, California, a company specializing in urban infill development and adaptive use. "He was very energetic and inspirational, and he had the capacity to draw out the best in the people around him. Part of my success is Don giving me the opportunity to do things that others wouldn't."

**Terner "had the capacity to draw out the best in the people around him."**

*BRIDGE*

Terner had that kind of incredible influence on people. They gravitated toward him, drawn by a combination of his vision, passion, and energy. He was an inspiration to many, even those on the other side of the ideological fence, including politicians and heads of corporations and institutions.

Deep down he believed that housing was central to people's long-term economic health and prosperity, which helped to grow individuals by moving them up the economic ladder and bettering their lives. In his mind, it was deplorable that people living in high-cost areas, who worked but could not afford housing, were vulnerable and excluded from having decent shelter.

BRIDGE Housing Corporation was a perfect fit for Terner. Under his leadership, the organization, from its inception in 1983 to his death in 1996, built nearly 6,000 units of housing in the Bay Area, valued at more than $600 million.

Among the projects was Marin City U.S.A., a $108 million mixed-use development with 340 units of owner and rental housing, a shopping center, parks, a library, and other amenities. It was Terner's pet project. It took more than ten years to revitalize the area, which had consisted mainly of public housing, sans retail services, in a low-income African American community.

**Terner "just wanted people to have decent lives."**

*BRIDGE*

Today, his protégé and former student, Carol Galante, continues to carry the torch at BRIDGE, overseeing the development of nearly 1,000 new units of housing each year.

Says Galante, the organization's president and chief executive officer: "Before BRIDGE came along, people thought nonprofits could only do small community projects. Don just turned that on its head and said it's not that communities shouldn't be involved, but we need companies involved to do this on scale. The organization was based on a real business model where we would be business people and not just look at this as a handout."

Terner insisted that BRIDGE meet three tests—quality, quantity, and affordability. It became his mantra, along with another: "Whatever it takes." And fundraising became his forte.

In 1994, Terner helped to crack open the biggest untapped source of new funding for affordable housing—pension funds. It was a huge coup. BRIDGE and World Savings and Loan formed the World/BRIDGE Initiative, a $340 million construction loan pool.

**"Don grew up with a lot of stability and appreciation for the American Dream of home-ownership. He just wanted opportunity for everyone, freedom from discrimination. He just wanted people to have decent lives."**

"He could persuade anyone to do anything—city councilors, bankers, neighbors. It wasn't just good logic and the power of persuasion. He inspired people to do the right things, whether they were students, staffers, or private developers," says Galante.

Alan Stein, the chairman of BRIDGE Housing, says one of the best meetings his group ever had was with the head of Chevron, George Keller. "His vision of affordable housing was drug related, with high crime—until he heard Don speak. To this day, he is one of our best supporters," proclaims the former secretary of business, transportation and housing for the state of California. "Don was just a driving force, and he was tough. He wasn't a hands-off guy. Everything we do at BRIDGE today is guided by the principles of Don Terner."

---

# Donald Terner

## BIOGRAPHY

D onald Terner—colorful, charming, and cheerful—did not take "no" for an answer. Convinced that providing affordable housing was a noble cause, he was relentless in his pursuit of supporters to fund low-income housing throughout the San Francisco Bay area. And more times than not, he was successful in obtaining the financing he sought.

His secret: "Don communicated enthusiasm and an ability to get things done, whether it was on the self-help level in New York, or at BRIDGE building a ton of housing around the Bay Area," says Chuck Laven. A former Terner student at the Massachusetts Institute of Technology (MIT), Laven is president of Forsyth Street Advisors, development specialists, in New York.

It was with that same level of commit-

*BRIDGE*

ment and determination that Terner left the United States in April 1996 as part of a peace and development effort led by U.S. secretary of commerce Ron Brown. En route to Bosnia, the plane crashed on a mountainside near Dubrovnik, killing everyone aboard. His family and friends say Terner, 56, died doing what he liked best—helping others. The only thing that mattered more was his family—his wife and kids.

Terner was born and raised in West Orange, New Jersey, the son of a small town, old-fashioned lawyer who ran a storefront family practice. His grandparents, European Jews, came to America to reap the opportunities that it offered.

"Don grew up with a lot of stability and appreciation for the American Dream of homeownership," says his widow and second wife, Deirdre English, a writer. "He just wanted opportunity for everyone, freedom from discrimination. He just wanted people to have decent lives."

Langley Keyes, a professor of urban studies and planning at MIT, first met Terner in Venezuela. At the time, Terner was studying at Harvard—where he earned three degrees—and working on prefabricated housing in South America.

"Don was a real 1960s type of guy," says Keyes. "He cared about a lot of issues. When he was working at MIT, he was very, very concerned about equity and low-income issues."

Terner had a burning desire to do a great deed for the world. In this pursuit, he did not avoid conflict, but he did shun jargon. He despised it and thought the affordable housing field was rife with it, particularly the U.S. Department of Housing and Urban Development. So he removed the words "households," "projects," and "people who earn 80 percent of the median income of the metropolitan SMSA [standard metropolitan statistical area]" from BRIDGE's lingo and replaced them with "families," "developments," and "people earning $12,000 to $25,000 a year."

Away from work, Terner enjoyed the outdoors and the arts. He was particularly fond of skiing, jogging, and swimming, but also loved the opera and symphony. Many years ago, between projects in Venezuela, Peru, and Argentina, he also briefly drove race cars and played professional soccer in Colombia.

"Don could have made three times as much money doing something else, but he didn't want to," says Alan Stein, chairman of the BRIDGE Housing Corporation. "He was always pushing to reduce the problems engaged in housing. He was an inspiration to the people who worked with him."

# CHAPTER EIGHT

# ROBERT VENTURI and DENISE SCOTT BROWN: Collaborating for Success

Mike Sheridan

## LEADERSHIP LESSON

### Stay centered.

"Analyzing others is knowledge.
Knowing yourself is wisdom.
Managing others requires skill.
Mastering yourself takes inner strength.

"Knowing when enough is enough
Is wealth of spirit.
Be present, observe the process,
Stay centered, and prevail."

*Tao, 33*

He is a writer, a teacher, an artist and philosopher, and a designer who has expanded and redefined the limits of architecture through his theories and projects. She is a planner, an author and educator, and an architect whose writings and projects bring long overdue attention to the relationship of architecture, planning, and social conditions. Both Robert Venturi and Denise Scott Brown—partners in life as well as in their award-winning Philadelphia firm of Venturi, Scott Brown & Associates (VSBA)—have changed the face and tenor of architecture and set its pace since the late 1960s.

Along the way, the pair has challenged conventional wisdom and stressed creativity and communication. Refusing to be labeled—let alone pigeonholed—Venturi and Scott Brown are constantly evolving, rethinking, and reinventing. They remain two of the most original thinkers in modern architecture, emphasizing that the business is not only about materials such as stones and steel, but also about ideas and concepts.

What singles out Venturi and Scott Brown as truly eminent leaders in the design world is that they encourage continuing questioning of the status quo, forcing students, critics, clients, and colleagues alike to rethink their positions on architecture. As Venturi's Pritzker Prize citation noted: "…He teaches us to look at architecture, all architecture—not just his own—with new eyes which may have lost their star dust but are certainly better focused."

**"Meeting with Denise was not unlike participating in a college seminar. Lots of questions, lots of exchange, and great mentorship."**

Nancy Rogo Trainer, a principal in VSBA who joined the firm in 1987, said Venturi and Scott Brown provide an environment in which people are always learning, and are constantly trying to figure things out. "Robert and Denise remember when they were young and they go out of their way to assist younger architects," says Trainer. "They also struggle hard to make good ethical decisions—what's good for their clients, what's good for the firm, what's good for their employees. They are honest with their feelings and are not afraid to speak their minds. Sometimes it may get them in trouble, but clients are much better off for having them speak freely and truthfully."

Adds Silvia G. Fuster, who interned at VSBA for two years: "Bob and Denise were my teachers long before I met them in person. As an architecture student, I was inspired by the chutzpah and elegance of their writings and built projects. Working with them I learned that their work is a reflection of two bright individuals who have known how to effectively channel their and others' 'natural forces.' This to me is a true example of leadership."

Venturi and Scott Brown are theoreticians and designers with a particularly broad span of interests. They pay careful attention to the relationship between design, planning, and the social arena, and they share a common bond in their view of architecture's mandates and possibilities. Yet they are unique individuals, each of whom has a distinctive way of looking at the world.

Architectural historian Vincent Scully has likened Venturi to the French architect Le Corbusier because Venturi is "an innovator, who is able to free himself from the fixed patterns of thought and the fashions of his contemporaries." Venturi has continually challenged the conventional. His understanding of the cultural context of architecture, admirers say, has allowed architects and users of buildings freedom to accept inconsistencies in the form and design of architecture, and the possibility to enjoy popular taste.

Richard M. Rosan, president of the Urban Land Institute, studied under Venturi at the University of Pennsylvania (Penn) and found his teachings provocative at the time. "He had a profound influence on my early thinking, leading me to a unique career. Rather than strip away allusions to history, Venturi urged the design community to celebrate history and draw on its influence to reintroduce architectural richness to the built environment. His work at Penn represented a watershed in the evolution of contemporary planning and design in the United States," Rosan says.

Through Venturi, Rosan got involved in urban design and development in New York City, where he was hired by Jonathan Barnett to work for the Urban Design Group. "We started attempting to understand all the forces that influenced design and development in that city. Now, four decades later, all of us are still struggling with understanding and managing a more complex world," Rosan says.

Venturi is known for his comment, "Less is a bore"—a response to modernist Mies van der Rohe's dictum, "Less is more."

**Venturi and Scott Brown work on the campus design plan for Tsinghua University in Beijing.**

*Venturi, Scott Brown & Associates*

Venturi's point was that modern architecture had become too simplistic, and that his own style could be whimsical. For the Bicentennial in 1976, he and Scott Brown created Franklin Court, a dignified remembrance for Philadelphians of their famous son. The architects located the memorial below ground; then, on the site of Franklin's long-gone house, they traced its outline via a steel frame, creating a "ghost" house.

Denise Scott Brown has admonished others to "Think before you judge," a maxim that has played a major role in the development of her ideas about design in architecture. Looking objectively at problems and considering the merits of unattractive but effective solutions can help designers expand their horizons, free them from aesthetic ruts, and amplify their creativity, she explains.

Venturi and Scott Brown met on the architecture faculty at Penn in the early 1960s, when they came together to help save the university's 19th-century Frank Furness–designed library from demolition. (Some 20 years later, VSBA renovated the massive circular brownstone building that is now the Fisher Fine Arts Library at Penn.) As academics, they taught classes, held seminars, designed projects, and authored articles. Their book, *Learning from Las Vegas*, coauthored with Steven Izenour, turned the architectural community on its ear by suggesting that "low art" sources such as supermarket parking lots, roadside commercial strips, and gambling casino advertising offered valuable lessons in design, and by showcasing what was considered the ugliness of North American everyday life, defining it as an artistic stimulus that designers could learn from.

**"They embraced questions and confusion, innovating, and challenging the conventional wisdom, yet providing me with the resources and methods to get at the answers."**

But it was the architecture that issued from their professional partnership that drew the most attention. Among other things, Venturi and Scott Brown became known for architecture steeped in popular symbolism. In their designs, cultural icons are exaggerated or stylized. Kitsch becomes art. One of Venturi's first projects to capture the attention of the architectural community was a house for his mother in the Chestnut Hill section of Philadelphia. The Vanna Venturi House began as a square with a simplicity that recalled the work of Louis Kahn. But Venturi chopped off two of the corners and pierced the others with diagonals. He then designed a great semicircular window and framed the two-story public rooms with gables. In 1989, the home received the American Institute of Architects' Twenty-Five Year Award as a design of "enduring significance that has withstood the test of time."

Venturi and Scott Brown have been chopping off the lid of architecture ever since they started. Founded by Venturi in 1964, their firm has worked on nearly 300 projects, in China, Japan, France, England, Italy, and all around the United States. Their work has included urban and campus plans and design competition entries, but its main body is some 140 completed buildings. Among them are the famous Sainsbury

Wing of the National Gallery of Art on Trafalgar Square in London, a capitol building for a French regional government in Toulouse, and a romantic resort and spa in a national forest near the shrine city of Nikko, in Japan. These, and 75 academic projects on 35 campuses—campus centers, libraries, laboratories, and campus plans—make a colorful display on www.vsba.com, a Web site that endeavors to explain as well as depict the work.

In their work, Venturi is, in general, in charge of architectural design, and Scott Brown of urban and campus design, as well as of the development of architectural projects that emerge from her campus plans. But their responsibilities overlap and they collaborate closely on most projects.

And each continues to learn from the other. Venturi has said that his appreciation, support, and learning would have been less than half as rich without his partnership with his fellow artist. There would be significantly less dimension within the scope and quality of the work, including dimensions theoretical, philosophical, and perceptive, especially social and urban, pertaining to the vernacular, to mass culture, from decorative to regional design and in the quality of our design where Denise's input, creative and critical, is crucial," he says.

Venturi and Scott Brown have tried to make their office a meeting place for a rich diversity of minds, whose thoughts can lead in many directions. They see attracting talented people and enabling them to work effectively to fulfill their personal and professional aspirations as profoundly important for the quality of their work. One of their many legacies to architecture is that they have, through the VSBA office, provided continuous stimulus for eager architect interns, serving as a kind of incubator and liberator for them. As a building is designed from the inside out and the outside in, so an architect must grow both from within, through training in the discipline of architecture, and from without, through the influence of persons and places.

"People, particularly architects, have the need, psychological and material, for support, for appreciation; and encouragement of this need is as significant for artists as for children in their development," explains Venturi. "As growing children need loving parents and supportive home and school environments, so artists need their supporters—trusting patrons and encouraging mentors, the latter sometimes via the work of artists of the past."

**Venturi and Scott Brown (sitting down, right and second from right), "embrace questions and confusion, innovating, and challenging the conventional wisdom."**

*Venturi, Scott Brown & Associates*

The pair provides remarkable opportunities to young people in their office. Says Fuster: "As an intern, I met directly with Bob and Denise on projects and I participated in all client and consultant meetings—not a common occurrence in most architecture firms. Meeting with Denise—with whom I worked much more intensively—was not unlike participating in a college seminar. Lots of questions, lots of exchange, and great mentorship. They set a climate of patience and respect for me, which diffused my fears of 'messing-up,' or of even trying for fear of making a mistake. They provided a context in which a young and relatively inexperienced person like me could think more clearly and make mistakes in peace, knowing that this is a healthy part of the working process. They embraced questions and confusion, innovating, and challenging the conventional wisdom, yet providing me with the resources and methods to get at the answers."

"The interns energize and excite us," Scott Brown explains. "Young architects have an 'oh wow!' attitude. They come up with lively ideas and suggestions and bring their high energy to our projects. Sometimes it's not easy to manage all that energy."

Venturi and Scott Brown know they must manage all that energy and also be good financial providers—yet as artists, simply making money has not been their bottom line. Architects, especially, have a difficult time with financial matters because often they undertake a project for the "sheer love" of it. The pair learned that grand ideas and great designs do not always provide predictable profitability. "Neither Bob nor I expected to find ourselves running a business," says Scott Brown. "As architects, we want to design beautiful buildings, but you have to be good in business as well as good in design. We have always been entrepreneurs and we love doing our own thing, but we must still know not only how to lead, but how to manage."

Scott Brown recalls that, by the early 1990s, their partnership had produced three major museums and received numerous honors and awards, but was looking ahead to bankruptcy. "We had some wonderful people working for us who deeply believed in the art of architecture and we did too. Then I found myself at dinner with the dean of a business school, who told me our problems were not financial but cultural. Our people believed that all Bob and I cared about was the art of architecture. He suggested we explain to them the requirements and issues of financial management and show them that we cared about this too—and particularly so if we intended, on occasion, to do work that was not profitable. So the next day we did just that. Then we all worked together to turn the financial problem around. We found that facing that situation inspired our staff— as architects, but also as business managers," says Scott Brown. "Now we have better financial systems in place."

> **"As architects, we want to design beautiful buildings, but you have to be good in business as well as good in design. We have always been entrepreneurs and we love doing our own thing, but we must still know not only how to lead, but how to manage."**

Always the teacher, Scott Brown believes in telling the members of her teams more than they, on the face of it, need to know about the project, so that, should they be required to make judgments without her, they will be broadly enough informed to be able to do so.

But the need to evolve new systems continues. VSBA's three recently appointed principals—Daniel McCoubrey, Nancy Rogo Trainer, and James Kolker—were once eager young interns. Over the past decade, a shift in management responsibilities has proceeded, slowly, in careful preparation for the continuity of the firm and the shifting of its legacy to future generations. As with all such planning, it is the intangibles of leadership that are the hardest to convey.

It might be a different way of looking at things, but then again Robert Venturi and Denise Scott Brown have always done it differently.

# Robert Venturi

## BIOGRAPHY

The man who would later become the thought-provoking *enfant terrible* of the architectural world had a happy childhood in which he was doted on by both his father and mother.

Robert Venturi recalls his parents keeping him well supplied as a small child with toy building blocks, and surrounding him with beautiful objects and good books. He remembers that, on one of his first trips to New York City, his father instructed the taxi driver to pull over at the old Penn Station on Seventh Avenue. The elder Venturi then led his son down the gallery that overlooked the great hall based on the Baths of Caracalla. Recalls Venturi: "I shall never forget the breath-taking revelation of that monumental civic space bathed in ambient light from the clerestories above." He also credits the influence of his mother, whose sound but unorthodox positions as a socialist and pacifist "worked to prepare me to feel almost all right as an outsider."

From those beginnings, Venturi went on to become one of the most original talents in contemporary architecture. He graduated summa cum laude from Princeton University in 1947 and received his Master of Fine Arts degree there three years later. He studied as a Rome Prize Fellow at the American Academy in Rome from 1954 to 1956, and then worked in the offices of Eero Saarinen on a number of projects, including the design of the General Motors Technical Center. He also worked with legends Louis I. Kahn and Oscar Stonorov in Philadelphia, and then turned to teaching architectural theory and being a studio critic at the University of Pennsylvania's School of Architecture.

In 1966, he published a thin but potent volume *Complexity and Contradiction in Architecture*, which became an extremely influential text that was viewed as an attack on the current Modernism. In the book, he posed the question: "Is not Main Street almost all right?" arguing for "the messy vitality" of the built environment. Venturi wanted architecture to deal with the complexities of the city, to become more contextual. Explained the author at the time: "We were calling for an architecture that promotes richness and ambiguity over unity and clarity, contradiction and redundancy over harmony and simplicity."

He met his personal and professional partner, Denise Scott Brown, while teaching at the University of Pennsylvania in the early 1960s. In 1972, he and Denise Scott Brown, with Steven Izenour, wrote *Learning from Las Vegas* (MIT Press). In 1996, Venturi's *Iconography and Electronics Upon a Generic Architecture* (MIT Press) was published, and Venturi and Scott Brown's latest book—*Architecture as Signs and Systems in a Mannerist Time* (Harvard University Press)—is scheduled for publication in fall 2004.

**Venturi and Scott Brown became known for architecture steeped in popular symbolism.**

*Venturi, Scott Brown & Associates*

# Denise Scott Brown

## BIOGRAPHY

When Denise Scott Brown was growing up in Johannesburg, South Africa in the 1940s, the city was a refuge for Europeans and a sophisticated center for the arts. Denise was particularly impressed by an art teacher named Rosa van Gelderen, a Dutch Jewish refugee, who told her: "You will not be a creative artist if you don't paint what's around you."

"She meant the life of Africans in the streets of Johannesburg; she made me look around me and awoke my interest in popular culture. I was about ten," recalls Scott Brown.

"Even at that time, no child in South Africa could be unaware of the issues of justice and equity between the races. And there were other issues: for example, their distance from the centers of European culture made South Africans feel out of touch," she continues. "Yet being at a periphery raised challenging artistic questions: Where did we fit cultur-ally—with Africa or with England? This brought up questions of 'is' and 'ought:' what environment, in fact, lay around us and how was this dif-ferent from what the dominant culture's media—for the most part English—suggested should be there?"

Seeking answers took the talented Scott Brown on a decades-long journey that still is not complete. In 1952, she left South Africa to work at an architect's office in London, later entering the Final School at the Architectural Association in London, in the midst of the "look back-in-anger" era—a time when society was in upheaval and social activism was part of education. Arthur Korn was her adviser, and through his teaching and his book *History Builds the Town* he showed Scott Brown how the social life and history of an era affected its building.

In 1956, Scott Brown worked briefly in Rome for architect Giuseppe Vaccaro. She returned to South Africa in 1957, then left for America a year later to enter the city planning department at the University of Pennsylvania (Penn), because renowned architect Louis Kahn taught there. At 29, her master's degree completed, she joined the faculty at Penn. At the time, Kahn was reassessing architectural history under the tutelage of a young architect, Robert Venturi. Scott Brown met Venturi in 1960 at her first School of Fine Arts faculty meeting, after she made an impassioned—and ultimately successful—plea to save the Furness Library. She recalls: "After the meeting, Bob introduced himself and told me: 'I agreed with everything you said. My name's Robert Venturi.' And I replied: 'If you agreed with me, why didn't you say something?'"

At Penn, Scott Brown set up a course of faculty lectures on theories of planning, landscape, and architecture, and ran seminars. Venturi taught the theories of architecture course that followed and they collaborated on his seminars. A public and private partnership was born.

When she joined Venturi in marriage and practice, Scott Brown was well known for her contributions to theoretical research and education on the nature of cities. Today she is known for a series on urban and university planning and development projects, which employ unique design tools that Scott Brown has evolved through a melding of the methods of planning and architecture. She notes with pride the Perelman Quadrangle campus center precinct at Penn, and the Palmer Drive Life Sciences complex at the University of Michigan. Under her leadership, both emerged through a process that moved seamlessly from campus planning to design. She is currently at work on the campus plan for Tsinghua University in Beijing.

CHAPTER NINE

# SAM ZELL:
# Investing in People

Desiree French

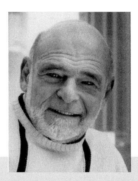

## LEADERSHIP LESSON
### Challenge the process.

"If we want people serving customers and making product to take ownership and responsibility, they will have to define and create the means for successfully living out those responsibilities on their own. There is much the top and the bottom need from each other to live out partnership, but top- and staff-defined competencies and training prescriptions only reinforce dependency and the bureaucratic mindset. If training is needed, and it will be, let those who require it define it, choose it and manage it. And let different units find different paths."

*Stewardship: Choosing Service Over Self-Interest*—Peter Block

In the late 1980s, when overbuilding and a pervasive economic recession hit commercial real estate hard, Sam Zell pounced at the opportunity to make a killing. The pioneering contrarian snatched up distressed properties across the country from over-leveraged owners and their lenders. For this, he was nicknamed the "Grave Dancer."

And dance he has, all the way to the bank. Today, the 62-year-old billionaire sits atop a massive real estate empire that is second to none. His vast holdings, now shared with millions through publicly traded REITs, or real estate investment trusts, make Zell the largest owner of leased property—office buildings, apartments, and manufactured homes—in America.

His private investment firm, Chicago-based Equity Group Investments, also controls a diverse array of businesses that, at various times, have included radio stations, cruise lines, restaurants, drug stores, insurance firms, and agriculture products companies—as well as a stake in the Chicago Bulls professional basketball team.

"What has set him apart is that he's such a global and strategic thinker. He's always focused on the next wave and positioning his company for these changes," says Stephen Quazzo, a former Zell lieutenant and now chief executive officer of Transwestern Investment Company in Chicago. "Sam is a master strategist."

This ability to predict market trends meshes well with Zell's strategic goal to aggressively compete in, and dominate, the commercial real estate market based on scale and a propensity for offering low-cost management and high-quality service.

Being a market leader has always been high on his list. And having the right people in the right jobs—and letting them run with the

**"Sam delegates responsibility, gives you a lot of rope, and allows you to take educated risks. There is nothing that he won't consider in the business environment if there is an opportunity and we can figure out how to take advantage of it. We just have to know the downside of the risk."**

**Equity Office's Bank of America Tower in Seattle.**

*Equity Office*

ball—has been as important to his growth strategy as buying properties on the cheap.

"He won't take someone under his wing and work with him day in and day out, but his door is always open," says Gerry Spector, executive vice president and chief operating officer of Equity Residential, which Zell chairs. "Sam delegates responsibility, gives you a lot of rope, and allows you to take educated risks. There is nothing that he won't consider in the business environment if there is an opportunity and we can figure out how to take advantage of it. We just have to know the downside of the risk."

In other words, Zell, who is widely hailed as an intelligent risk taker, does not micromanage. He lets his top people execute. But when it comes to vision and direction, the buck stops at his door.

In Zell's book, leadership means never having to take a vote. "If you have to take a vote, you've lost because you are not 100 percent sure that everyone is with you. You lead by example, by instilling in other people a desire to follow your example. A true leader is able to encourage and develop a following based on substance, not authority," he says. "If I have an idea, I want people to want to follow it. If I have to tell you what to do, I've lost. Being a leader means being able to convince people that an idea is meritorious. That is leading, not directing."

Zell says he is both a leader and an entrepreneur, the latter of which requires an appetite for risk. Thus, his is a corporate culture deeply rooted in an entrepreneurial mind-set, and irreverence. Zell does not cower before traditionalists or straight business types, and his executives are encouraged to challenge authority, speak up, and ask questions when necessary. Feedback, not blind leadership, is the order of the day—coupled with a very healthy dose of fun. The environment is one in which people's differences are accepted, and all egos are checked at the door.

Audaciousness and openness, coupled with Zell's strategic thinking, have gotten him, his employees, and his companies far. When portfolios become available that meet the mass and scale he desires, Zell, ever the optimistic deal maker, buys them, deftly incorporating them into the nation's two biggest REITs—Equity Office Properties Trust and Equity Residential—both of which he chairs.

In fact, Zell built the two companies from the ground up and also has an interest in two other REITs: Manufactured Home Communities, Inc., which owns mobile home parks, and Capital Trust, a real estate specialty finance company.

> **"If I have an idea, I want people to want to follow it. If I have to tell you what to do, I've lost. Being a leader means being able to convince people that an idea is meritorious. That is leading, not directing."**

Equity Office owns such trophy properties as One Market in San Francisco and Rowes Wharf in Boston. It is the nation's largest publicly held office building owner and manager. Originally made up of four funds created by Zell/Merrill Lynch, it went public in 1997. Since then, Equity Office has nearly quadrupled in size through strategic mergers and acquisitions totaling more than $17 billion.

With nearly 700 properties and more than 120 million square feet of office space in 27 major metropolitan markets, Equity Office is the largest office REIT in the country and the first real estate company to be named, in 2001, to the Standard & Poor's (S&P) 500 index. Its market capitalization is a whopping $25 billion.

Equity Residential, as the largest publicly traded owner and operator of apartment buildings in the country, is equally impressive. Also now on the S&P 500, it has more than 200,000 units in more than 950 apartment communities nationwide. Its market capitalization is $15 billion.

Equity Residential also invests plenty of time, effort, and money in staff development. For three consecutive years, it has been listed among the top 100 companies in America for employee training. Last year, it took third place in the American Society for Training and Development's 2003 Best Awards for excellence in training and human capital development.

The success of both Equity Office Properties and Equity Residential is mind-boggling. In Zell's mind, bigger provides a platform to be better. Having two REITs on the S&P 500 has contributed enormously to the acceptability of REITs in the overall marketplace.

**Equity Office's 161 North Clark in Chicago.**

*Equity Office*

"This is a new frontier, to create public real estate companies of this scale that have the potential for tremendous operational synergies. They [Equity Office and Equity Residential] are well positioned to consolidate what is a fragmented market," says Hoke Slaughter, head of U.S. Real Estate Investment Banking at Morgan Stanley. "Sam's legacy is bringing real estate into the corporate mainstream. He has shown that management can be fully aligned with shareholders and that major real estate companies can be run in a transparent manner, both of which are critical from an operational and capital markets standpoint."

But there is another Zell legacy, and it focuses more on the human side: instilling a sense of adventure, excellence, and entrepreneurial flair in his workers, and getting a disparate group of employees to act as one.

The latter has become increasingly more difficult to do in today's business environment because the scale of the business has changed dramatically. Organizations are now so huge that a leader's influence has become much more diluted. But Zell seems to have it under control.

"He was always able to take complicated issues, synthesize them, bring them down to their base level, and really simplify them," says Quazzo. "He's a motivator. He's never been one to shut down an idea, and that's very empowering. I've taken his 'be accessible, be open-minded, and listen well strategy' to heart."

> **"He's a motivator. He's never been one to shut down an idea, and that's very empowering. I've taken his 'be accessible, be open-minded, and listen well strategy' to heart."**

# Sam Zell

## BIOGRAPHY

James D. Harper, Jr., was an executive vice president of Continental Bank in Chicago when he first laid eyes on Sam Zell in 1974. It was a day he will never forget. "When I first met him," recalls Harper, "he was in a jumpsuit and a gold chain."

Zell, a valued bank customer at the age of 32 and a gifted entrepreneur, had his own unconventional dress code. Today, his clothing of choice is a notch better—jeans and polo shirts. But at that first meeting, Harper was impressed. "He was very intelligent, one of the best world-class negotiators I've run into."

Now 62, Zell got an early start. One of his first business ventures was taking snapshots at his eighth-grade prom. He also resold copies of *Playboy* magazine to schoolmates at a 200 percent markup.

Zell first indulged his interest in real estate by managing off-campus student housing during the 1960s while a student at Michigan University. Before long, he was buying up small apartment buildings and converting single-family housing into multifamily units. Even then, Zell was convinced that he would be successful—much like his father, a jeweler with an appetite for clinching property deals.

Zell earned an undergraduate degree in political science and a law degree at Michigan University. He practiced law for exactly one week. "I just didn't think it was a good use of my time," he says.

Zell's roommate and fraternity buddy at school was Bob Lurie. Zell formed a tight bond and business partnership with Lurie that spanned nearly 30 years, until Lurie's unexpected death from cancer in 1990. The twosome bought local properties and never looked back. They later diversified out of real estate and began buying companies and investing in sports teams. The synergy between the two was flawless. Zell acted as the rainmaker, working the investment community and scouring new opportunities. Lurie worked the office, handling day-to-day operations and keeping the peace. After Lurie died, Zell brought in more people to fill Lurie's role, a move that freed Zell to continue doing what he does best—negotiate the deal.

"At a bare bones minimum, it's always interesting and challenging to be in a deal with Sam. He has a very forceful personality that at times can be a little irreverent. He's not necessarily in conformity with the general wisdom," says Richard Saltzman, president of Colony Capital, LLC, who worked with Zell on the Zell/Merrill Lynch funds years ago. "He's clearly willing to take risks, but calculated ones, with a real view as to what the risks are and how they can be managed."

Risk-taking spills over into Zell's personal life. He is an avid skier, racquetball player, and motorcyclist. Zell's Angels, a club of motorcycle buddies that he leads, tours Europe and Asia, and members even have their own jumpsuits and leather outfits.

A known prankster, Zell is also quick to send unique birthday gifts to friends, including a bagpiper and dancers.

The only thing he doesn't do "is thrust himself into the limelight, not that he doesn't like having a good time," says Thomas E. Dobrowski, managing director of Real Estate & Alternative Investments at General Motors Asset Management. "He is noted for throwing a party every now and then in Chicago and inviting his friends. It's always a spectacular event."

Associates and friends say Zell is very focused, inspirational, and a great storyteller. He never seems to tire of speaking to students at the University of Michigan, the Wharton School of Business at the University of Pennsylvania, and Columbia University.

"His legacy is not so much individual mentoring, that's not his long suit. It really is the vision he brings of the entrepreneur," says Harper, president of JDH Realty Company in Miami. "It's a gift when you can get young people excited and [encourage them] to take risks for the reward. His gift is a tremendous ability to motivate people."

Around the first of every year, Zell sends 600 to 700 friends a sculpted gift with an accompanying message set to music. Each message has as its theme an enlightened message on the economy. "Sam has been doing it for ten years now and each one [gift] seems to get more elaborate," says Dobrowski.

This year, the message theme focused on global outsourcing and how the Internet is making it easier to outsource work. "His ability to call industry trends can be downright scary," says Hoke Slaughter, managing director of Morgan Stanley's Investment Banking Division in New York City. "The lead time for producing and distributing these gifts must be at least a year. So he's making his call a year in advance. When he conceived of "Wired Exports," global outsourcing had not really hit the radar screen—now it's a topic everyone is talking about. To me, that's an indication of Sam's vision as an investor."

**Zell (right) with Richard Kincaid, president and chief executive officer of Equity Office Properties; and Marsha Williams, executive vice president and chief financial officer.**

*Equity Office*

# Appendix 1
# Bibiliography

Bennis, Warren, and Joan Goldsmith. *Learning to Lead*. New York: Basic Books, 2003.

Block, Peter. *Stewardship: Choosing Service Over Self-Interest*. San Francisco: Berrett-Koehler Publishers, 1993.

Buckingham, Marcus, and Curt Coffman. *First, Break All the Rules: What the World's Greatest Managers Do Differently*. New York: Simon & Schuster, 1999.

Cashman, Kevin. *Leadership from the Inside Out*. Minneapolis: TCLG, llc, 1998.

DePree, Max. *Leadership is an Art*. New York: Bantam Dell, 1989.

Dreher, Diane. *The Tao of Personal Leadership*. New York: Harper-Business, 1996.

Harkins, Phil. *Powerful Conversations: How High Impact Leaders Communicate*. New York: McGraw-Hill, 1999.

Jacobson, Ralph D. *Leading for a Change: How to Master the 5 Challenges Faced by Every Leader*. Burlington, Massachusetts: Butterworth-Heinemann, 2000.

Loeb, Marshall, and Stephen Kindel. *Leadership for Dummies: A Reference for the Rest of Us*. Foster City: IDG Books Worldwide, 1999.

Kouzes, James M., and Barry Z. Posner. *The Leadership Challenge*, third edition. San Francisco: Jossey-Bass, 2002.

# Appendix 2
# ULI Leadership
# Development Initiative
*Identifying best practices and sharing experience*

The Urban Land Institute is working with human resources professionals and leadership development experts to create a variety of opportunities for members to develop their skills and to craft a comprehensive leadership program for their enterprises. A number of tools have been developed both for those beginning their careers as well as CEOs of growing companies.

### CEO Roundtables

- Annual, for-fee, invitation-only forums for CEOs, COOs, HR VPs to share best practices.

### Continuing Education

- Offer members' companies custom education options (e.g., Deloitte, CB Richard Ellis).

### Fall Meeting and Spring Council Forum (meetings.uli.org)

- Personal development speakers and session audiotapes.

### District Council Workshops

- Summer Retreat.
- District Council Day at the Fall Meeting.
- 2005 SelectLeaders Workshops.

### Executive Coaching Center (executivecoach.uli.org)

- Clearinghouse of resources—e.g., assessment, coaches, review course, resume writing services.
- Knowledge database for young professionals on career management.

### *Urban Land* Magazine (urbanland.uli.org)

- Community Builders Profiles—a series on those who have made a difference in their hometowns.
- Trustee profiles—every month, a ULI trustee is featured in *Urban Land*.

### Leadership Essentials Audio Programs (leadership.uli.org)

- Interviews with authors and experts—produced quarterly, available as CDs and tapes at ULI Bookstore.
- Online archive available to ULI members to listen to or download.

### Publications

- Lassar, Terry J., and Douglas R. Porter. *The Power of Ideas: Five People Who Changed the Urban Landscape*. Washington, D.C.: ULI–the Urban Land Institute, 2004.
- Olson, Josh. *Better Places, Better Lives: A Biography of James Rouse*. Washington, D.C.: ULI–the Urban Land Institute, 2003.
- Ewald, William Bragg. *Trammell Crow: A Legacy of Real Estate Innovation*. Washington, D.C.: ULI–the Urban Land Institute, 2005.
- Galatas, Roger, with Jim Barlow. *The Woodlands: The Inside Story of Creating A Better Hometown*. Washington, D.C.: ULI–the Urban Land Institute, 2004.